MW01295715

Surviving The Douchebag Apocalypse

How To Recognize, Understand, And Deal With Jerks, Manipulators And Bullshit People

Edward Carboni

outskirtspress

DENVER, COLORADO

The opinions expressed in this manuscript are solely the opinions of the author and do not represent the opinions or thoughts of the publisher. The author has represented and warranted full ownership and/or legal right to publish all the materials in this book.

Surviving The Douchebag Apocalypse
How To Recognize, Understand, And Deal With Jerks, Manipulators And Bullshit People
All Rights Reserved.
Copyright © 2014 Edward Carboni
v3.0

This book may not be reproduced, transmitted, or stored in whole or in part by any means, including graphic, electronic, or mechanical without the express written consent of the publisher except in the case of brief quotations embodied in critical articles and reviews.

Outskirts Press, Inc.
http://www.outskirtspress.com

ISBN: 978-1-4787-2256-4

Library of Congress Control Number: 2014903508

Outskirts Press and the "OP" logo are trademarks belonging to Outskirts Press, Inc.

PRINTED IN THE UNITED STATES OF AMERICA

Praise for *Surviving the Docuhebag Apocalypse*

Edward Carboni nails it again in his sometimes funny, sometimes grave, but always nakedly accurate treatment of the state of humankind. With laser guided precision and the brilliant light of truth, Carboni pierces the bullseye with three purposeful nonfiction arrows.

This tight, efficient volume reassures readers that we are not alone in the world of the self-absorbed and shallow—those who suck the energy from a room and drive others to prescription medications. And then, very gently, the author provides a no-nonsense blueprint for setting oneself free from the forces of evil—the douchebags. But the third hit-on-target is the lodestone of the work. Carboni reminds us that we all have the *"douchebag gene"* and challenges us to manage those impulses that drive us to be the douchebag in the lives of others. *Surviving the Douchebag Apocalypse* is at once a lively report of the things we think and dare not say, and also a telling mirror of Snow White lore reminding us of our participation in a society speeding toward the ridiculous.

Carboni galvanizes the rawness of Hunter S. Thomspon, the wry wit of Bill Bryson, the strategy of Niccolo Machiavelli and the insight of Ayn Rand in his comedic, vernacular tirade. The language is barstool authentic, but the message is anything but pedestrian. If I owned a bookstore, I wouldn't know on which shelf to display this book. It's self help, it's humor, it's business and it's the hot ticket I would want right on the counter.

Prepare yourself to laugh, clench your fists in anger and breathe many sighs of relief when you get on the path to *Surviving*. I thank the author for treating me to an advance read of the type-script for he set me free from the bonds of the douchebags in my life and forced me to guard against and suppress the *"douchebag gene"* that resides within us all.

G. Buck Manning
Author, *Pirates of the Whirling Dervish*
Key Largo, Florida
January, 2014

Other Titles By This Author

Cinderella Joe -A novel

Published by America Star Publishing

Boss Ralphie -A Holiday Tale of Redemption

Published by Outskirts Press

All titles are available through your local bookstore or directly from the publishers as well as Amazon.com, and Barnes and Noble.

No douchebags were injured during
the production of this book.

For Krystal

Contents

Introduction

You know them. They are your friends, co-workers, family members, bosses, boyfriends, girlfriends, customers, neighbors, etc. They are the people in your life that act in ways that makes your head spin, or keep you in a perpetual state of angry disbelief. They are douchebags, and they can fuck up your day, your week, or your life.

In this particular age of social media, reality T.V., and the celebrity craze, more and more people want to be famous, to have power or control over others, and to be in possession of some reputation of greatness. But this is also the age of the superficial persona; an age where less and less people feel any real need to earn these things. Our culture is a breeding ground for douchebags, the denizens of a 'never-never land' where they always get what they want and never have to grow up. We hold these shallow values high in this instant-gratification world. And along with it, along with all the Jerry Springer shows, Tweets, Facebook 'likes', selfies, personal blogs, twerking and affluenza, has come the proliferation of the douchebags, now more than ever, in an abundance of apocalyptic proportions.

These are the people who are so full of themselves that they defy explanation. We are exposed to legions of them, and they boggle the senses. They are the people with an overvalued sense of self-worth and importance or an overbearing opinion of things they know nothing about. They are the people who drive you crazy because they never seem to make sense to anyone but themselves.

And you're fed up. You've had enough but you don't know what to do. They insert themselves into your world based on a false façade they presented at the outset, one that later proves to be absolutely based on dubious information and misdirection. So it's time to rid your life of them…if not actually physically, then at least mentally…which will take their power to upset you away from them. It's time to set yourself free.

This book will explain what douchebags are, how they think, how they dress and act and speak, so you'll be better prepared in the future to repel their insertion into your life or simply be able to sidestep social entanglement with them. This book will also give you strategies for dealing with douchebags you already have in your life. It will explain that there is a little douchebag in us all, and how to keep it at bay. A true douchebag is some-one who exhibits *prolonged, repeated, and persistent* behaviors and mannerisms of the type explained herein. Although we all act like douchebags from time to time, being a genuine douchebag requires consistency, so you may want to allow a little leeway for friends and family who you think are such creatures; they may ac-tually be going through a tough stretch on the road of life and not 'livin' la vida douchebag'. This book will explain the douchebag mentality, so you can understand what's really going on in their twisted psyches. Not that you want to understand them, just understand why they are the way they are. Knowledge will set you free! So…let the healing begin!

1

What is a Douchebag?

"A pejorative term for an arrogant or obnoxious person."

-Wikipedia

Well spoken, wiki. But even though this definition gets to the point, it does not come close to covering the spectrum of what a douchebag is and what they do. So many people go thoughout their days dealing with these people and somehow get trapped in some sort of relationship with them. Like snow flakes, no two douchebags are alike. Each has their particular mudus operendi. Here is a small sampling of some of the typical practices of douchebags you may know.

They keep a vigilant eye on others. There's no better way for a douchebag to make themselves look better than to point out the mistakes or shortcomings of others in front of a grateful audience. It feels good to them to focus on the faults of other people, and others will appreciate their keen sense of observation. Whenever and wherever, a douchebag will revel in publicly showing fault in others. For them it's an opportunity to build up their fragile self-esteem.

Their opinions are handed down by God. What a douchebag thinks about anything isn't just a perspective, but the perspective of the most intelligent being in the universe. The douchebag isn't afraid to share them loudly with everyone. And if someone dares to respectfully disagree with their opinion, chances are they will become angry and hurl insults at the digresser. After all, the douchebag did them a favor by allowing them to witness the inconceivable brilliance of their twisted psyche.

They exaggerate everything. Not to be daunted by silly little facts that get in the way of their brilliant assessment of any situation, your typical douchebag will blow anything out of proportion so as to have the most dramatic rendering of any event. Facts are for the weak minded who do not have the magical ability to create mountains out of molehills. That is their true power, and they wield it with force.

Appearances are the supreme measure. Forget about the truth; what's really important to a douchebag is how they look on the surface. As long as the douchebag can convince others how compassionate and kind they are, others will be more willing to overlook their true nasty, malicious, and selfish nature. By this manner, they can give friends and business associates the shaft, and they'll never see it coming. Remember, it's not about faking it 'till you make it for a douchebag; it's about faking it 'till they can fake it again.

Their anger proves the veracity of any argument. When fact and reason fail, douchebags just get angry. Most people are not aware that anger is one of the most common ways that people express insecurity and fear. So a douchebag will probably get angry with everything, especially petty and small things, and in that manner they will be showing the world exactly what they are: weak-minded and trivial.

They simply just lie. Beyond exaggeration, which is a twisting of the truth, douchebags will eventually get down to the meat and potatoes of what they really are all about, and just plain lie right to your face. For them, the truth can be boring and very confining, so at some point they will set themselves free. They don't bother with truth when they have a vast universe of lies to choose from. To truly be an effective liar to others, douchebags need to be effective liars to themselves. They will cling to a rigorously-fabricated collection of grandiose fantasies that define the real them that never was. Let's say they want to be a doctor – forget medical school; they'll just tell people they're a doctor! See how easy it is? Bam, now they're a doctor! When people call them on the stupid shit they say or something they did, a douchebag will just lie about it. They would rather swear upon the souls of a morgue full of dead relatives that they would never say or do whatever it is they did say or did do. That will make others think they're the crazy one, when in truth it's the douchebag who is batshit over the top. Douchebags will get angry too, and use phrases such as "how dare you" and especially "do you know who I am?" because that will just give dramatic proof to the truth of their lies.

Complain. Again, the opinion of a douchebag is handed down by God, so when he does't get his way (and of course his way is *the* way), then it's time to complain. Complaining is a wonderful way to let others know when things don't meet his expectations. There's no need for the douchebag to express his expectations beforehand; people should know already. Whether it's the government, or that the supermarket doesn't carry his favorite brand of...whatever, he will complain excessively. Occasionally, the uninitiated may try to explain to the douchebag that some situations "are what they are," and the douchebag won't be fooled by anyone who tells him anything along the lines of *doing something* to change a situation. He has complained! And like a magic wand of 'what the fuck', he has exposed to the universe how things should be.

Deny responsibility. Events that don't serve to strengthen her fabricated and delusional reality require the douchebag to completely deny them. She will not allow anyone to hold her accountable for her actions. She will remember those who do this to her. She knows that these people are just trying to make her look bad out of jealousy. She will be sure to punish such behavior to show the people around her that it is unacceptable for them to hold her accountable for her words and actions.

Embrace the drama. Inside, the douchebag is a frightened sixteen year old-girl regardless of gender or age. He has an unending need to draw attention to himself, and to effectively get it he needs to cuddle up close to the dramatic. He's loud. He needs to let the whole world know the important thoughts that go through his mind. He cuts off people in conversation. He makes up realities that fit his own world view. He's dramatic in everything he does and says—drama makes everything so much more real and interesting. In the end, remember, it's all about him.

These are but a few of the many traits of the douchebag. The douchebag in your life may or may not exhibit one or all of these traits now. But they will eventually. So be ready…it's a comin'.

2

The Sign Of A Douchebag

It would be nice if all the douchebags we've ever met had come into our lives wearing a sign that simply states 'I'm a douchebag'. But in the course of life, this ain't gonna happen. But what we can do to spot a douchebag is to be vigilant and patient and allow them to show themselves before getting involved. Douchebags abhor patience. They know that thoughtful consideration of any kind will not bode well for them; it goes against their flash-over-substance existence. Here are a few physically obvious indications that you may be dealing with a potential douchebag.

Keep in mind that these signs are not *always* indicative of a douchebag, but they can serve as a way to help you keep your guard up. So don't automatically label someone a douchebag because they show these signs, but you'll be ready if they are, and it will take away their element of surprise.

Their mode of transportation

"Everyone realizes that people who are so needy for attention they dress up and be as loud as possible are you guys and sixteen year-old girls."

Cartman to a Harley biker gang
in the South Park episode, *The F-Word.*
-Matt Stone and Trey Parker

There is nothing inherently wrong with an appreciation for a well made and well performing mode of transportation. But for the douchebag, it's much more than that. To them, the vehicle they choose to drive is an embodiment of something they don't really posses. The vehicle represents an 'image' they want to 'project'. They attach their identity to the image, and bolster it at every turn. In turn the 'image' becomes a laughable charade: a charade the douchebag has absolutely no clue about. A few good examples are the Harley Davidson motorcycle and the Hummer SUV. There is nothing wrong with either vehicle, and both are probably the best or close to the best as far as mechanical engineering is concerned. And it's not even the attire that is sported by Harley riders, or the lack of any need for driving the Hummer in any terrain where it is completely unnecessary, e.g. Southern California or South Florida.

The reason these two particular vehicles are noted is not because of any physical reality of the vehicles, but rather it is the douchebag's sense of himself while riding or driving one. The Harley guy needs attention in the form of "I'm going to act like a completely obnoxious asshole who wants people to be 'uncomfortable'" when he revs his engine unnecessarily loud and for long periods of time. For him, it's attention...attention mostly likely not given to him by his parents in his youth, so he needs to extract it from everyone else around him. To avoid this particular douchebag, you just need to keep away from where they congregate. They tend to be cheap (except when what they are purchasing items for prersonal display), so avoid cheap places of business. If you have to deal with them, remember, the persona is an illusion, and illusions cannot be maintained for a very long period of time. It's useless to confront them on it—as useless as telling a child dressed as Spiderman for Halloween that he's not really Spiderman.

As for the Hummer driver...and his brethren in such vehicles as the Chevy Corvette, the B.M.W. and the Porsche, they are birds of the same feather. These are fine automobiles. There is no questioning the value of engineering or rugged performance that these cars possess. The problem is not the particular attributes of the vehicles but rather the attributes the drivers of these vehicles impart to themselves. Not all are douchebags, but the douchebaginess of the vehicles is apparent. The Hummer douchebag driver sees himself as one who is in 'command'. He can do as he pleases, regardless of how it impacts anyone around him. The rest, relegated to the sports car douchebag clique, simply want to be seen as more than what they are. It's a pathetic attempt to raise their stature without possessing the required internal structure. As with the Harley douchebag, it's an attempt to join the masquerade of social acceptance. So remember, it does not necessarily mean that the driver of any of these vehicles is a douchebag, but they are tell-tale signs that one could be in your presence. Gird your loins when around them, so as not to allow them the 'in' that they so desperately need to feel a sense of power in this world.

How they act and dress

A douchebag is primarily concerned with maximizing attention to themselves. More to the point, they are wholly concerned about getting attention; it's their drug of choice. And the attention, even when they're making a complete fool of themselves, is so addictive to them that they hardly even know. A douchebag has no problem dressing like a 20-something at a frat party, even though he is well into his 50s. Your female douchebag, being as shallow as she was when she was 20, will still wear the same revealing clothing at 45 that she wore then, even though nature and time have long since said "no, please…please don't".

There are some douchebags who live and die by fashion. Expensive suits and gowns are the things they cannot live without. To them, clothes do make the person, but it's only because in their case there's really very little of note inside, so the outside needs to be as spectacular as possible, before others realize that they simply are a stain on the human fabric.

A douchebag is also discernable by the conversation you have with him.

Eleanor Roosevelt once said: "Great minds discuss ideas; average minds discuss events; small minds discuss people." The douchebag, as you probably already know, talks about himself. Constantly. Incessantly. Regardless of the topic of conversation, the douchebag will somehow bring it back to himself. Sometimes the urge is so strong to do so, that he will completely cut you off in mid-sentence. Usually this only comes after time, after he has secured some form of upper-handedness or acceptance in your relationship with him. Before then he will act as though he is listening attentively, hanging on every word you say, while in reality he is not listening at all, unless you are revealing something that he can use against you at a later time. It's just part of the act to let you know what a great listener he is, an attribute most people find attractive in others. Most of what you say is going in one ear and out the other. But his goal here is make you *believe* he's listening.

Most people do this from time to time. When we encounter persons who are simply venting or just talking out of their ass, we act polite to avoid an argument. But the douche bag—well, the douchebag has an agenda. You have something he wants, be it physical, emotional, or monetary, so he needs to get in your good graces before the trap is sprung. One good way to tell if someone is giving you the douchebag ear-service is to ask questions about the conversation in a reasonable amount of time after it has ended. If he seems like he's hearing it for the first time, well then it's because he is hearing it for the first time.

The doucebg, gaslighting and selective memory

Dealing with a douchebag is a bad idea on any level of human endeavor. Usually we do it in a state of not knowing, or we do it in a state of human sympathy, telling ourselves, 'they're just going through something' and, as an unwitting pawn, we put up with a lot more bullshit than we have to. One of the more profound, and for the douchebag, probably the most fun way to gain control over others, is by utilizing their ability to transform reality into a douchebag friendly environment. The douchebag does this first by testing the water in order to find out how much he or she can get away with in a small-scale innocuous situation. Gaslighting is a douchebag favorite for this.

The term 'gaslighting' is a derivative taken from the early 20th century film 'Gaslight', where a woman's husband tries to make her think she going insane to get her money by, among other means, turning the gaslight down. When the wife makes note of this, he says she is seeing things. It seems small, but over a prolonged period of time it can cause a great deal of psychological harm because it makes the recipient of such treatment question their own sanity and it helps the douchebag see how far their powers of persuasion can go to make others question their own senses.

Obviously, since gaslight is no longer in use, the douchebag will have to resort to other means, which could be anything, and depending on the nature of your involvement with the douchebag, could have devastating effects. If the relationship is a business one, watch out—it's gonna cost you money. If it's a romantic relationship—it's gonna cost you much more. But before you get involved, remember that the signs of such things will be evident. In business, if there were rumors that you heard, ask questions before signing anything. Watch the reaction in a potential business partner. If indignant outrage is the response, walk away from any deal, it's a sham and the reason the douchebag is outraged is because he's been found out. If the douchebag soft shoes, hold off for a while, cite concerns, and wait until things seem a little clearer before committing any finances. Use your gut and above all, practice patience.

If the relationship is romantic—you're screwed depending on the level of your involvement. You married a douchebag? Now you have problems. You're dating a douchebag? Fewer problems, but still a problem. You've met a douchebag? Well, you probably don't even know it. But you will soon enough. In the end, you just need to use your instincts. They are telling you the truth. And they are the mortal enemy of the douchebag.

An ounce of prevention

The objective here is essentially to have a checklist of behavioral clues that will help you from being led on by a douchebag at the outset. What you need to do is not to judge a book by its cover, no matter how good that cover looks. Get a few pages into the book before you purchase it, metaphorically speaking. It's always good to remember that a douchebag has little more than the cover. For the most part, a douchebag is a shallow superficial individual who is trying to make the most of appearances for his own benefit. It would be nice if the douchebag walked into your life wearing a clown suit and wig, tooting a rubber-ball horn all the while. The fact is they don't. So you have to look a little closer.

Some obvious signs

Louder than he has to be: For a douchebag, what he is saying doesn't really matter so much as the fact that he's talking and all other conversations are subordinate to his. This is a free throw, because it demonstrates a lack of presence in, and awareness of, the surrounding environment—a truly douchebag trait.

A vehicle of compensation: This was addressed earlier, but can't be overstated enough. This has typically been relegated to the mid-life crisis douchebag, but it really is a universal signal, the signal being 'I need to prove something to others.' This could be anywhere in range from the Porche, to the Hummer, to the latest hybrid eco-friendly vehicle driven by those who want others to be well aware of their ceaseless efforts to save the world. Each is potentially driven by a douchebag. So if you see them coming, keep your guard up until you get a better measure of the person.

Obvious fake tits: This, combined with other verbal clues to be discussed later, can be a great litmus test. These aren't the kinda boobs a girl would get to compensate for a dearth of mammalarity, but rather an augmentation of stunning disproportion. A real test of the douchebaginess of the owner is if she insists they are real. Fake tits can be a sign of a need for attention and a dearth of self-esteem. They are also the silent mating call for the male douchebag who is highly motivated by large breasts. A recent study has concluded that men who are attracted to large breasts are more prone to objectify women and to be hostile to women (Verin Swami and Martin J. Tovee, 2013).

Wears sunglasses in the dark: This 'so cool I don't even need to see' behavior is a douchebag staple unless the individual is playing a musical instrument on a stage. Otherwise, the wearer is trying – desperately – to prove his coolness. And it does work, but only with other like-minded douchebags.

Carries himself with a defiant attitude everywhere, usually with arms folded in a disapproving manner: The individual posing in this manner is waiting for something to comment about negatively, when the truth is that the negativity is only in himself, and he is waiting like a Venus fly trap for someone to venture within speaking range so he can spew forth his venom about something that is making him unhappy.

Wears everything Harley: Although this is not a dead ringer, it can be. Stay sharp.

Wears everthing Harley, wears sunglasses at night and carries himself with a defiant attitude everywhere with arms folded in a disapproving manner: It was stated earlier that the douche-bag doesn't go around dressed like a clown honking a rubber-ball horn. But this is exactly the aforementioned clown.

Too much gold: Wearing jewelry is not a dead ringer sign, but those who wear excessive amounts may be trying to prove something. Another subtle clue with the over-bejeweled type is while wearing excessive amounts of gold jewelry, the wearer is excessively cheap. It pretty much shows that their focus is primarily, or worse, exclusively self-involved.

A Speedo: Unless someone is an Olympic swimmer or from Eastern Europe, there is simply no need for anyone to be wearing one of these. It is, as will be discussed later, a shock-value attention-seeking choice of clothing.

3

"a tale told by an idiot, full of sound and fury, signify-ing nothing."

> Macbeth, Act V, Scene V
> -William Shakespeare

"Better to remain silent and be thought a fool than to speak out and remove all doubt."

> -Abraham Lincoln

Now that we have a handle on some of the possible physical types of your garden variety douchebag, we now move from what they look like to what they sound like.

There are some words and phrases that are indigenous to a douchebag, things that they cannot resist resorting to. To a douchebag they are the equivalent of verbal gravity; an irresistible force dragging them down to their natural level. These should be used as signposts to you, pointing the direction *away*. Be aware of them and you will avoid an unneeded moment of drama, and escape relatively undamaged.

Douchebags will impose their opinion in every situation: If there's a defining characteristic of a conversation with a douchebag, then the 'unasked-for opinion' is a benchmark. The douchebag has an overwhelming need to express himself in the form of an opinion, and usually it is an opinion based on sketchy or usually non-existent facts. These opinions are articulated with the douchebag's signature aloofness. They have, in one verbal fell swoop, defined something that they really don't know shit about. The fact that they don't know shit about what they are talking about but need to talk about it is due to the douchebag's propensity for 'emotional intellectualization' a process where a douchbag confuses some insecurity for a thought process, or it could stem from his need to be right about everything, which serves to foster his reputation (in his own mind) as the most intelligent person alive.

The douchebag's favorite word— 'I': No matter what the conversation, or the circumstances, the douchebag is unwaveringly compelled to bring the conversation around to himself. This is not a subtle tactic, as it will be done with force and need. For the douchebag, a conversation that doesn't revolve around him is no conversation at all. You'll be able to recognize this instantly. This is truly a give-away signal. When you know the conversation does not necessitate the ruminations of the individual invoking his own self into it, and he *persistently* does so, then you know you're most likely dealing with a douchebag who doesn't have the slightest clue that every conversation is not a therapy session. Which he should be going to – regularly.

Beyond 'I', douchebags have a fanciful and fabricated history: Douchebags, deep inside somewhere, don't like themselves very much. It is inherent upon them to change who they are...but only in a superficial way. The story they tell of themselves will be a fantastic tale with little or no facts to back it up. Most people don't question what others say simply for the reason that most others wouldn't fabricate a past history out of nowhere, but the douchebag lives on such things and will do so until his true ineptness is exposed, and only then do people begin the long road of confirming the past of the douchebag. If you have any dealings with someone you think is a douchebag, be careful of the fabricated resume. To them, their highly promoted self is the real self, and not to be questioned. If you have to question them, be sure to be in possession of the facts before you expose them. But typically, once again, this an invitation for you, as Bugs Bunny would say, to "exit – stage right."

Douchebags talk about others: When douchebags are not engaged with puffing themselves up in some fashion by their constant self-talk, they will usually be talking about others, and they may even know some of the people they talk about. When a douchebag speaks of others, you can be certain that most or all of the talk will be negative. The douchebag experiences this talk in the same way as his never-ending talk about himself bolsters him up and makes him feel good. This is the other side of their coin—feeling good about themself by putting down others. They may be strangers or, if they didn't see it coming, dear friends.

To make it even more fun, the typical douchebag enjoys throwing people under the bus who, in some way, are in possession of a quality that they wish to possess but never will. For them it is a form of competition, a competition that must be won at all costs, because the douchebag sees himself in competition with… everyone. Whether it's a perception that someone has a better car than his, or someone lives a lifestyle that the douchebag envies. Whatever it may be, the douchebag feels an internal need to put it down, because by comparison, he senses in some way that he holds the shitty end of an imaginary stick.

Douchebags make judgments based on incomplete or unsubstantiated facts: For the douchebag, one of the greatest and most fulfilling ways to project their twisted sense of the world and to bolster a sense of well-being is to know what is going on at all times. The douchebag will judge everything, and he will do this immediately upon receiving either a visual sighting, or simply in the midst of conversation. He will define things based (as if this was a surprise) upon either what he would do, or as a way of putting down something or someone that he perceives as a threat. One very common example would be if a douchebag's girlfriend is having a conversation with another man. The douchebag perceives that the other man is trying to pick her up. At the same time the douchebag's massive sense of insecurity (she could do better than me) sees a situation where his sense of himself is being compromised, and…well, you know what happens next.

Douchebags will say whatever is needed to win an argument: An argument here does not mean a heated emotional debate (although it could turn into one), but rather a discussion of differing opinions. For the douchebag this is truly a fight for survival. Even if the argument is in private, the douchebag feels that his appearance is in jeopardy, so he needs to be right to maintain his illusion of himself. There will be no facts left untwisted or simply fabricated that will stop him from this end. The need to maintain his perception of himself is so great that every argument has the gravity of a title bout. It has nothing to do with reality, just the douchebag's perception of himself.

Douchebags will try to point out your faults, which will be his own: When in the midst of an argument with a douchebag there may come a point where his argument becomes untenable, especially if he is around more than one person who refutes the douchebag's position (this is also why the douchebag likes one-on-one conversations over group discussions—he can better control one-on-one conversations). For the douchebag this is as good as a small death, and not the French meaning of the phrase. Faced with a loss that will minimize the douchebag, he will go on the attack. Just as a wild animal would do if cornered, the douchebag will fight for his life. Remember that the douchebag is what *he thinks* others perceive him as, and not what others really perceive him as (think "The Emperor's New Clothes") and being cornered he will attempt to drop his douchebag nuclear weapon, which will be a vicious personal attack on the person or persons who have dared to diminish him. It is simply a subterfuge of conversation. He needs to win and fight himself out of his own mental corner.

4

What the Douchebag Does

It's time to examine what really makes a douchebag shine in all their jerk-off glory. If you were unlucky enough not to see or hear the signs of the douchebag at the outset, then you're in for a real treat, because now the douchebag is in, and like the vampires of old…you let him in, and he's not so easy to get rid of. Here are a few tactics you will encounter when dealing with a typical douchebag.

Manipulation: For a douchebag, manipulating and controlling others is a hallmark of their nature and, to them, the central hub of their powers (yes, a douchebag will imagine he has special powers over others). When you first met the douchebag in question he or she seemed to be an easy-going, carefree individual, or exuded confidence. Maybe he or she was fun and gregarious—the life of the party. But after a period of time, you noticed subtle changes in behavior and attitude. You just chalked it up to him or her 'going through something,' and shrugged it off; after all, during the early courtship or friendship, they let you know how fun or confident or caring or deep they were. But now it's all different. You question the things they say, but then dismiss the questioning.

You ask yourself why the fuck anybody would do something like that. The douchebag will give advice (really just more manipulation) so he can get whatever he wants at the time. He will try to control others' behaviors to better suit himself. He will engage in deceptions, either verbal or physical, designed to maximize the fulfillment of whatever his desires are. Compliments will come at you so underhandedly you would think you're playing softball. And all the while, in a public space, they seem just like the person you knew at first. But in private, it's a different story.

Subversion: Trust is the cornerstone of every personal human interaction, be it business, freindship or romance. To the douchebag, trust is a leverage tool he keeps handy at all times. Once you've trusted the douchebag with personal information, especially anything negative or anything that could have adverse effects for you, you will be treated to yet another form of manipulation—subversion. It's the douchebag's way of training you not to question the things he says or comment about the things he does. Once he has 'the dirt' on someone, he will disseminate it when it suits his purposes the best. The more highly skilled douchebags will not even need 'the dirt'…they'll simply make up what they want and disseminate that. He will, of course, do this in a way that you won't see coming, will have no time to prepare for the aftermath, and will spend weeks or years trying to overcome.

When you share personal details of an unflattering nature with a douchebag, it's probably one of the few times he will actually pay attention. He's gathering ammo to use for the time when he feels he'll need it most. And when he needs it, he'll disseminate it in private conversations with those he knows can do the most damage to you or your reputation.

Martyrdom: Another method the douchebag uses to gain control over some situation, is to play the martyr. He or she (most likely) can climb upon a cross of personal misery in a New York minute. This type of douchebag is actively looking for something to be disappointed with, hurt by, or insulted by. This can be done by a douchebag you know or one you've just met. If you know this douchebag, then you're so sick of this kind of bullshit that you ignore it outright, but if you don't, chances are good you're gonna get sucked into their overemotional tar pit of hell—more on this later.

Emotional Intellectualization: For certain douchebgs, the difference between thinking (considerate postulation of a situation) and feeling (base emotions of fear or insecurity) are indistinguishable. These douchebags make up realities based on what their fear tells them, and this type of activity can easily be spotted and identified. Whenever a douchebag inserts himself into any situation (and he will—he's a douchebag, it's *all* about him), and personalizes it, he is using emotional intellectualization. The douchebag cannot tell the difference between an event and its impact on him. For the douchebag, there is no difference. An example would be a person who knows a particular douchebag and walks into a crowded room and does not see the douchebag and engages in conversation with others. The douchebag instantly assesses the situation and will conclude that the other person is *actively* ignoring the douchebag. This would be a situation where the douchebag feels diminished in some way, and depending on the nature of the relationship will make the other person pay for it. The douchebag, being the center of all, could never possibly be missed being seen.

Expectation: If there's one thing a douchebag has in overflowing abundance, it is expectations. And these expectations almost always center on others doing something to benefit the douchebag. Rarely will you hear a douchebag talk of challenging themselves to be a better...whatever. They are already perfect; it's the world that needs to adjust to them. The most fun part of the expectations of a douchebag is that they are always changing. What they want in moment one is not what they want in moment two, and here's the best part...you should have known.

Overstepping bounds: The douchebag knows the best way to do anything; he's a master who lacks only two things...knowledge and experience. He knows the best way for you to do your job (they've never done it before); they know the best way to fish (they never catch shit); they know the best way to succeed in business (they've failed at everything). In short, the douchebag has a resume of things they've never done that you could learn from, and they are never shy about telling you so.

The other kind of douchebag that oversteps bounds is the one who wants authority but not responsibility. They want things done their way but shirk when things don't turn out right. They tell you their opinion (you didn't ask) on everything. They are overbearing in conversation, and controlling of it. They are smug and may have just enough authority to make your life a pain in the ass if they want to, and they often use the aforementioned subversiveness to be certain you do not challenge their authority as a jerk-off.

Taking things out of context: Even though the douchebag may be an intelligent person, they just don't think quite right. They take any situation and, in the douchebag way, will completely change it to fit very nicely into their twisted mindset by inserting themselves, which of course puts them at the center of the action. It's a lot like the martyr quality of the douchebag, except that this particular character trait does not need an actual event, they'll simply make it up, leaving you to do the puppy dog head-tilt in response.

Needing to 'win' at everything: Being a douchbag isn't always easy, and for most of them, the need to prove their superiority over others is a constant and pressing matter. Their insecurity demands proof of their superiority. This is done by winning. Now there are some who see a competitive nature as a form of confidence, but to a douchebag it's a way of proving who he is (which he never was) at every turn. In an argument with a douchebag you will encounter mostly verbal sleight of hand and a change of the central argument to fit the direction the douche-bag is headed. If he's winning, he'll continue on the same track. If he's losing, he will twist the subject around to something he thinks he can win at. In this mode the douchebag sees himself as being clever, while others see him as being an asshole. One thing is for sure; don't plan on winning any argument with a douche-bag. For you, it's a discussion of ideas. For the douchebag, it is nothing short of the survival of his image, and to a douchebag, his image is all he has.

If you are in any competition with a douchebag, the chances are pretty slim that he will follow any kind of rules, and therefore the douchebag will always have the upper hand. If you're involved in anything competitive in conjunction with a douchebag, there will be heady days of victory, followed by an inevitable downfall that will bring you down with him.

Lacking empathy: Of all the fun facts about douchebags, this one is a great huge neon sign coupled with trumpets and fireworks. The douchebag does not have the ability to see things from the point of view of anyone else…ever. His mindset is universal, and others who do not see things that way only cause consternation for him. From the things he likes, to his political viewpoint, he sees everything as what he thinks it is. He is horrible at seeing when someone is having a bad day; he sees only that his needs are not being met. When his attention needs are not being met, he has no understanding that others do not instantly and immediately recognize these needs, so the douchebag will act out…well, like a douchebag.

They have selective memories: For the douchebag, the need for a grand reputation that is often based on illusion usually runs up against the vast and overwhelming needs of his insecure nature. In this dichotomy, the douchebag will act in ways that are completely contrary to the story he tells. Both the actions and story are spokes of the same wheel of not being enough. These actions usually show the douchebag for what he is, a selfish and self-centered child who wants his toy, and he wants it now. The problem, if you are involved in any way with a douchebag is that when the time comes for a reckoning of his actions, the douchebag will simply deny it. This keeps his multi-colored balloon of reputation aloft while getting no closer to the bottom of events that had transpired. This is a lot of fun to watch…from a distance, but it is a source of mental and sometimes emotional torture for those around the douchebag. And to make it even more fun, the douchebag will consider anyone who brings up such actions as an individual who is trying to destroy his reputation.

They rage: Rage is the big daddy-Grand Poobah action that a douchebag engages in. This may come across as simple anger, but it really is an expression of deep seated fear of losing the bubble of illusion the douchebag has created for himself. The rage is a quick-lit fuse that burns furnace hot and is, to say the least, fucking frightening. For the douchebag, it's a response to some embarrassment or a response to his creation of himself that is in the midst of being found out as false, and the flake-headed douchebag cannot handle it. For him, the delusions that run around his head are the truth. At this point, the douchebag cannot resort to his selective memory because some evidence is publicly displayed that would refute his illusions. The douchebag fights back with anger that resembles the 'fight or flight' instinct of a trapped animal. He is fighting for his very life, and that's the life he has made up in his own mind. If the douchebag in your personal world is violent…watch out. If he's not, the storm will soon pass and his protestations will be ample evidence of his culpability. And even more fun…he'll probably relegate the rage episode to his selective memory. He'll simply forget it ever happened. And you will too, if you know what's good for you.

They are not always a douchebag…on the outside: Deep down inside the douchebag knows what he is. He knows he has a childish nature and a self-centric view of the world even if he may appear to be knowledgeable, intelligent, kind hearted and generous at times. Even though this deep internal knowledge is there, he also knows it must be hidden from others at times to get what he wants from them. These are the actions that either get you involved with a douchebag or keep you around them. He does these things at great strain, knowing full well the inner jack-in-the-box asshole that constitutes his true nature is waiting to come out and play. He knows that his true self will not be accepted or tolerated for very long (people tend to simply walk away from an asshole when they show themselves at the outset of any social encounter). So he works very hard to demonstrate his kindness, his generosity, his sympathy for the less fortunate, but all the while his inner Obi Wan Kenobi of the Jerk-Off Jedi Knights waits for you to buy into his bullshit.

5

A not-quite historically correct line-up of some of history's more famous douchebags.

Douchebags have been around since the dawn of civilization. Before civilization, there was simply the hunter-gather whose sole intent in the world was survival. Survival depended upon using all mental facilities to procure the basic…really basic… needs of humanity at the time. Food, water and shelter equaled survival. Small groups of humans were mostly mobile; traveling where the food went in the seasons. This ended with the advent of collective agrarian systems—and with the spawn of the village came the quintessential village idiot. But more importantly came the douchebag. No longer was cleverness needed for simple survival—that was assured with herded animals for meat and milk, and crops that were cultivated on farmlands. This new situation promised, at least for periods unprecedented by their hunter-gatherer predecessors, a steady supply of food. In conjunction with these cultivating and herding techniques, humans built towns of which some became cites, and then, after a measure of comfort set in—they started engaging in the most recognizable of human behaviors and started killing each other over stupid shit. Most of the killing sprees were fashion related, where a group wearing blue was deemed to be showing off, incensing the red wearing group to the point where it was decided the blue-dressed people had to go. These fashions were known as religions, one of the main bastions of douchebagery. After that came government, another form of religion that simply had no god, but boy did they have rules. The rules were made by those in government so that they could be broken by wealthy merchants who 'subsidized' government officials and also by those in government who felt they were above everyone else. From the first collectivization of humanity through the advent of the Fertile Crescent in the Middle East, the Greeks, the Romans, the Dark Ages, the Renaissance, and the age of the Automatic Coffee Maker, the douchebag has had what he has needed to flourish—a collective system where his true nature could hide and lie in wait until he could manipulate others for his own gain. Here's a small sampling of some of the great douchebags of history.

Cain, the first douchebag: Cain set the standard for douchebags. He killed his brother Abel because he became jealous that God favored Abel's sacrifice of livestock over Cain's sacrifice of agriculture. Cain didn't know that God had a thing for lamb chops at the time, and so Cain took it personally. Not having the balls to say to God, "Yo, God...what the fuck?" he did what is now considered to be the douchebag playbook staple: he whacked his brother, hid the body and lied about the whole thing. At this time in human history, God was 'hands on' with people and called Cain on the situation, saying "Yo, Cain, what the fuck?" God doesn't do that sort of thing much these days. The lesson: douchebags have an overwhelming tendency to deny facts that make them look bad, regardless of how culpable they are.

Rameses, the Pharaoh of the Exodus: It is highly unlikely that Rameses was the Pharaoh at the time of Moses, but for the sake of this discourse, he'll do. Rameses was the guy who wouldn't let the Israelites out of slavery, and he's a douchebag because he followed the classic douchebag principle of ignoring the reality of a situation (a situation that lessens his ego) even when the repercussions of this course of action will be very fucking bad. After the frogs and the pestilence, and especially the river running red, the guy just couldn't get the clue that shit was going to get a lot worse before it got better. He let his arrogance, pride, and ego dismiss an undeniable reality (in the story), and the consequences were that so many lambs were slaughtered for threshold blood that many lamb chops went to waste. Oh, and yeah, a few people died too. The lesson: douchebags don't like losing (it makes them look bad), and will tend to be apt to lose all instead of walking away.

Critias, the guy who had Socrates put on trial: When a douchebag faces opposition to practices and statements that he needs others to believe in order to maintain control of them, then that opposition needs to be done away with. Socrates questioned everything and therefore the man just had to go. The lesson: a douchebag *needs* others to believe the bullshit that they spew, and if you oppose them or catch them in hypocrisy, you're gonna pay the price.

The Sadducees at the time of Christ: This group of Judaic rulers at the time was the representative of the conservative religious and political (and wealthy) class in Palestine. They no more represented the Jewish people than right-wing Christian freaks represent the works of Christ today. These were the guys in charge of biblical law, and it was a law that only they (as they told everyone) could interpret. Jesus being the guy who didn't quite agree with what they were saying, they had him whacked at the hands of the Romans. Lesson: A douchebag (or a collective group of douchebags) cannot tolerate dissension. It gives people bad ideas, even worse ideas than spray-on hair. And these ideas can challenge the authority of those who have power over others. The lesson: if you disagree with a douchebag, watch out. You're making them look bad by pointing out their hypocrisy.

Caligula, the Roman Emperor: Before he went batshit crazy, Caligula started out as a simple douchebag. One story of his self-obsession was that due to a receding hairline and hair loss, he ordered that none in his court could have hair longer than his. Among many of his other exploits was an extreme sexual perversity that had no bounds and could not be sated. At one point, he worked to have himself declared a god. Now that's megalomania! He was also the first Roman Emperor to be killed by his own personal guard. The lesson: Douchebags will do whatever they think is right for themselves at every moment, not considering there will be moments after when others around them decide that they just are not going to put up with their shit anymore.

Henry the VIII, King of England: A very well documented account of what happens when a douchebag doesn't get what he wants when he wants it is Henry the VIII. In his particular case, he couldn't get a woman to bear him a male heir so he blamed the women. When he couldn't 'switch horses' at his convenience to achieve this end (there was some pesky religious tenet against divorce), he just got rid of that religion and got himself a brand new one. He also had his exes killed so they couldn't tell anyone what a bad lay he probably was. The lesson: when you get into bed with a douchebag, whatever illusions they have, you better be ready to make them come true...because a sharp axe awaits if you don't.

Mussolini, Hitler, and Stalin: The three stooges of death, destruction, and mayhem. These guys collectively created such an indelible era of human cruelty that it's hard to imagine. Of the three, Mussolini was the Curley—or rather the Curly Joe. But it was his example that inspired Hitler and his Third Reich, which inspired Stalin and his purges. But the connecting thread of all three of these guys was their thoughts of grandiosity about themselves. Each perceived themselves as some kind of either savior, reviver of a lost empire or in Stalin's case, a paranoid freak who rewrote history as it suited him (mostly because he had many in that history killed). The lesson: A douchebag has such a huge ego, they think they can do things that they can't. But a douchebag's power lies not in the fact that he can do something, but rather in the illusion he presents that he can. In the end, when the proof of the pudding comes around you will find yourself a lot worse off than you ever were before.

Saddam Hussein: A very good example of a modern-day douchebag. Even before he invaded Kuwait, he was an asshole with little ability and a ruthless nature (always a bad combination) and a delusion of military might (the mother of all battles). He also had a personal concept of victory and defeat. When, in the first gulf war, the allies complied with the NATO-mandated goal of free-ing Kuwait and stopped their attack on Iraq at a certain point, Hussein claimed victory. This victory was seen by him only on a personal level. He was still in charge, so therefore, he won. That is until about a decade later when he emerged from his spider hole expecting to 'negotiate'. The lesson: a douchebag sees everything from a personal lens and a personal lens only. And quite a rosy lens it is. The dead and wounded in his army, if they could speak, would probably have had a different view of the affair.

The Westboro Baptist Church: These guys are what you get when you combine homophobic grandstanding with what seems to be inbreeding. It doesn't appear to be that the goal of this particular group has anything to do with the teachings of a guy named Christ any more than Chicken McNuggets have to do with…chicken. To them, 'God hates fags' is a perfectly reason-able assessment of the true nature of the Supreme Being of the universe. And to spread this message of love, what better venue than the funerals of soldiers who have died in combat. The lesson: Douchebags like controversy and attention. When they do not get enough of it, they will create it.

6

A Situational Douchebag Inventory

Unless you work in retail, rarely is a douchebag encountered out of thin air, materializing as a specter from some otherworldly plane to stand before you to wreak havoc in your life, just like the idiot on a plane who just can't help but make a loud emotional scene over some insignificant detail just before the sky marshalls haul his ass away. Rather, they are the people who have come into your life wearing many different hats. They are friends, co-workers, relatives, customers, partners, parents. They are those with whom you have a emotional conection—be it hate or love—or those where there is no connection, just a seething loathing seeking an outlet. Here are but a few of the situations in which you may encounter or are dealing with a douchebag. The list is woefully incomplete, but you'll get the idea.

The parental douchebag: Let's face the facts. Nobody grows up in the Brady Bunch. Unless you remember the episode where Mike Brady comes home late and liquored up after having to deal with his incompetent staff at work, an overbearing boss, and the young receptionist who, without words, is a constant reminder to Mike that middle age is not creeping up on him, but has crept past him. While sitting on the couch finishing off the last drops of a bottle of scotch, he sees the budding Marcia stroll through the living room, and he remembers that Marcia is *not really* his daughter, and ensues in a drunken seductuion that eventually ends in divorce and disgrace.

Of course there's no episode such as that, but wow, it would have been a ratings giant. The point is, parents are the first examples of how to live life, and continue to be throughout your life. For good or bad they are the example of how to act, how to feel, how to think. The problem is that not all parents are cut from parental stock. A douchebag parent is one who seeks their own fullfilment or gratification through their children. Some want their children to be just like them and to define their child's view of the world through their eyes and limit the child from discovering things on their own. They see their children not as individuals with different desires for their lives and a different skill set than the one they possess, but rather as replicants of themselves. They desire their children to have the same world view as they do, a world view that they never question in themselves and feel confident that it is correct.

In the form of advice, a douchebag parent will not suggest that their child think through a situation and make the choices that would be best for them. The douchebag parent will simply tell their children what they would do in that particular situation, regardless of what the outcome would be. For this kind of parent, imitation is flattery. These are the parents who never really grew up emotionally. The ones who still have a twisted image of themselves as being in their teens, with the same set of glossed-over yet undeveloped social skills as they had then. These are the parents who could never admit little Johnny would ever do such a thing in school. These are the mothers who have no problem letting their little girl dress up like a $40 whore for the prom. They wish they could dress up like the $40 whore they are inside and go to the prom themselves. These are the parents who don't realize that their children need boundaries and guidance, not a best buddy. The reality is that the parent needs a best buddy, and who would you want to be your best buddy? That would be the person who you've trained to be just like you, wouldn't it?

The fact is that douchebag parents are trying, in a myriad of ways, to live vicariously through their children, either pushing them into things that the parent would like to have done in their life, or pushing them from the perspective of their own undeveloped sense of themselves.

The other form of douchebag parenting is the abusive parent. These are the parents who have a stringent view of how their children should look, speak, and what they should do. Failure to do so results in some form of abuse, either emotional degrading or physical abuse. What the douchebag parent is saying in these situations is that the child has made the parent 'look bad' either in their own eyes or the in the percieved eyes of others. A douchebag cannot handle looking bad, either in themselves or by proxy with their children, who are to them simply an extension of themselves. The point is that more times than not, it is a douchebag parent who molded the core behaviors of the douchebag people we meet today.

Douchebag parents also use martyrdom as an effective tool. This is extremely effective because of the emotional nature of parent-child bonds.

The douchebag relative: A douchebag relative can be one of the toughest douchebags to deal with. They're in your family. They're hard to avoid. Any conflict causes family drama. But they're still fucking douchebags. They will tell you how to live your life, what you should do with your money, and how to raise your kids. At family gatherings they will bring themselves and nothing more, except for the unexpected guest that you are supposed to accommodate. And they will stay much longer than planned (or much longer than *you* planned). The douchebag relative always has a scheme to 'make a fortune', but never the funds to get it started, which of course, is where you come in. The douchebag relative's life meanders from one emotion filled crisis to the next, along the way delving into the deepest of romances (they met a week ago in rehab). The wedding is tomorrow, and they are truly shocked when it ends badly, which prompts the need for some funds 'to help tide me over'. They were a troubled teen in their youth and stay a troubled teen well into middle age.

The douchebag boss: Is usually a source of much consternation. They are simply the idiots in charge. The douchebag boss sometimes doesn't know what exactly your job is, but he will not hesitate to tell you how to do it. His moods are unpredictable and you never know where the next rageful rant is coming from, or when it's going to come. The douchebag boss is the first to find fault with your work and the last (if ever) to find favor. He likes suck-ups (who cup his balls and tell him he's great) and deem beneath him those who do not. He's had some of the best dumbest ideas you have ever heard, and like the emperor who had no clothes, you better not be the one to say so (negative attitude). He has grandiose ideas with little to no implementation or organization but go through with it anyway, turning the office staff on their ear trying to figure out what exactly it is they are supposed to be do-ing. And when the bad idea falls flat on its face, there is either no mention of it again or the only mention will be how those below him failed in the execution. Bringing it up only puts your ass in the crosshairs. Working for a douchebag boss is the sure way to never get ahead, unless you are in the 'sphere of bullshit' where the circle-jerk never ends. Just gonna put your head down and work hard? Forget about it. If you do well, you're probably just going to show up the morons who cling to the douchebag boss to curry favor, and that good job you did will just be seen as a mark of someone trying to sneakily get ahead.

The douchebag co-worker: Stellar resume, impeccable refer-ences, well groomed. Yes, the douchebag hire has it all. And after the ninety-day grace period, those attributes will all vanish like the smoke they were. The douchebag employee needs a job. The reason he most likely needs a job is because he fucked up the last one. Eventually they come in late every day, do a half-assed job, leave early and complain the whole time about what a shitty place they work at. They are the poison pills in a work environment that drains others and makes people not want to be around them or communicate with them. Communicating with a douchebag co-worker is challenging. You want answers—they want to tell you how they feel, and the best part is how often they tell others how great they are at what they do. The douchebag co-worker is a back stabber, getting ahead by pointing out the faults of others, and never taking responsibility for their own. The douchebag co-worker will always have a definition for everything you do. They will define you as overwhelmed, in a bad mood, slacking in your duties. All these things will be brought to the attention of someone where they can do the most harm to you. Rarely does a douchebag co-worker tell you to your face (unless it serves to build them up at the immediate moment). Even better than that (as if it could get better) is when the douchebag employee sucks up to a douchebag boss. It's the *'When Harry Met Sally'* of 'what the fuck, how bad can this get?'.

The douchebag customer: Anyone who has worked in customer service, retail, food service, or any job that required interaction with the public, will have no problem affirming that people can be assholes. Typically douchebag customers are individuals who want what they want when they want it, or they have the direct intention of getting something that they are either not entitled to or something they do not want to pay for. They abhor waiting in line (they are too important), they *demand* special treatment (because they are special), they have no trouble creating drama scenes (needing attention), are sensitive to their perceived appearance (have a grandiose sense of themselves), and have no ability to understand that what they want when they want it may not be possible (lack of empathy). These, like all other douchebags, can ruin your day or week…if you let them. It is best to remember that the needs of the douchebag customer far outweigh any possible thing that you can do for them, so once the demands reach the realm of the surreal, stay focused on what you *can* do and simply disengage from them. You will not win and you will not break even, so mentally walk away. It's the best you're going to do.

The douchebag neighbor: Your goal in the neighborhood is to try to get along with everyone, to extend the hand of courtesy to your neighbors as you would like them to do to you. Your douche-bag neighbor, however, has other plans. His job is multifaceted. He is the shit-stirrer extaordinare who somehow needs to draw lines between anyone he feels doesn't fit his exacting standards of how things should be. His gossip is constant and the problems he has with neighbors are always evident, at least as far as his mouth goes. He is always vigilant and on the lookout for any infraction of a social code that he has implemented himself. He sees himself as the guardian of the 'hood, calling out others for whatever in-fractions suit his mood. If he doesn't like your landscaping, that landscaping is an 'embarrassment' to the entire neighborhood. He is in constant competition with his neighbors over any su-perficial thing he can find. He deems his home to be the best on the block. His possessions are paraded to show their incred-ible value, from a riding mower to the state-of-the-art sprinkler system. He spares no expense in describing them to you…you, who couldn't give a fuck about them. His put downs of others in the neighborhod only define his lack of self-esteem and need to make enemies of those who threaten his fragile ego. Most put up with it simply to keep the peace, and because those who stand up to him find more trouble than they bargained for. His advantage in the game he's playing (and usually, he's the only player) is that the neighborhood is the place where we live, a sanctuary of sorts, where we come home to and do not need the political and egotistical bullshit that we deal with everyday at whatever place we call work. But the douchebag neighbor is typically a pariah at work and the only way he can feel that he has some control in his life is to be overbearing in the relative peace of the neighborhood. Don't get on his bad side, or it's you who will be the topic of conversation over the fence.

The douchebag friend: First, understand one thing…a douchebag friend is no friend at all. Although they appear to be so and put on a certain show in public, the douchebag friend has no friends, except himself. Your role in the friendship is to do two things: one, never bring up anything that would make the douchebag look bad in a social setting. He has spent hours upon hours of time playing a role that makes him out to be the most loyal of people, the most trustworthy and steadfast of acquaintances. He has honed this act to a fine edge, and you are to respect it. When the actions of the douchebag friend are in direct contradiction to the things he says, your job, under the peril of reprisal, is to ignore the contradiction, especially in public where his own perceptions of himself hold sway.

Typically a friendship involves caring for each other, and sometimes it involves telling a friend he has, for example, a booger hanging out of his nose. But the douchebag friend sees it differently. Your telling him he has a booger hanging out of his nose makes him look bad in a very superficial way, and superficiality is the paragon of reality for a douchebag. He will look upon you with disdain and he will get you back. Your pointing out a simple fact has brought about a defensive and self-conscious reaction. To a normal person, helping a friend realize something is amiss is usually understood as an act of kindness. To a douchebag friend, you have simply made him look bad. The entire situation for the douchebag revolves not around the reality that there was something amiss, but the fact that you pointed it out. The bigger the social booger hanging out his nose that you tell him about, the bigger the reprisal.

The second job you have as being a friend to a douchebag is that of support. It is almost the same as the first part of your job, but this one involves allowing the douchebag to entertain whatever dramatic fantasies he has and to be supportive of them. This is critcal, because your non-consent equals opposition in the mind-set of a douchebag. This cannot be tolerated and you will pay.

Another trait of the douchebag friend is that they have no loyalty. To a douchebag anything you tell them will be twisted to make themselves look good to others. Anything they say to you is an effort to make themselves look good to themselves, so don't trust what they say or tell them anything of a personal nature. It's a waste of your time. Don't look for supportiveness or compliments from a douchebag, unless it is in a situation where they can glean admiration for their appreciation of the good works of others. A douchebag friend has no loyalty of confidence and will look upon your admission of failure in only one light...it makes him look better. A good example of a douchebag friend is the character Iago in Shakespeare's classic play, Othello.

The douchebag leader: The douchebag leader can be described as a typically self-appointed, self-promoting champion of some cause or group of people. They are CEOs of what some people call 'The Grievance Industry'. Their job, as they see it, is to be publicly outraged at anything and everything that goes against their cause, whatever that cause may be. They rarely hold any other position except for that of being the leader of whatever. Their stated goals are always vauge, but their media prescence is always clear. The true nature of these people is not to really advance whatever cause they aspouse at the moment, but rather to maintain their own positions of power and celebrity, never really promoting actions that would truly change a situation. They maintain their leadership role by maintaining *the need* for their services, whereas true changes would make them irrelevent.

The douchebag lover: The douchebag lover is much like the douchebag friend except their means of control are emotional ties. Once the infatuation has set in there will be a marked change in personality, a definitive role reversal that you didn't see coming. Why? Well, in the beginning of the courtship the douchebag is playing a role, and that role is to get you to fall in love with a choreographed image the douchebag carefully crafted. The douchebag will look for signs of what you like and present them as inherent qualities in themselves, at least for a short time until the goal has been met. Once you've made some move or conveyed some sort of emotional connection, that's when the douchebag comes out of hiding like a fucked up jack-in-the-box from hell. You never saw it coming, because the douchebag knows how emotions work and uses that knowlege to their advantage. And once you're in, it's hard to get out.

Feel free to mix and match these types of douchebags. They are interchangeable and the only constant is that after a superficial start, or from the outset, they all turn into jerk-offs.

7

And then there are the douchebags we encounter who have some stated purpose, some dire and all consuming agenda that they need to push upon everyone else; an agenda that trumps reason and understanding in favor of dogma and closed-mindedness.

The right wing conservative douchebag: In the eyes of the right-wing douchebag…conspiracy hangs at every turn. These are the people on the radio or next to you at the deli counter who see the world lined up against them, ready at any minute to take away their rights, tax them into oblivion or force them them to get out of their luxury SUV by rising gas prices (another conspiracy). These are the people who believe it is their God-given right to be able to sell anything on the market that makes them a profit, regardless of its worth. They are the hypocritical bible-thumping assholes who can blather about family values mere minutes after banging a fourteen year-old Thai boy in the ass. The conspirators are out to get them. The country is going to hell in a hand-basket. They believe in guns for all, and condoms for none and champion the unborn, as if they were personally involved, which they will be until the child is actually born and then the chant of no more welfare begins. Their morality ends when profits are on the table, then all the bible verses seem to vanish as their inner pirate comes out.

The left wing liberal douchebag: The left wing liberal douchebag is the oversensitive and overemotional guardian of our social conscience. In their often failed social experiments they forget that the world is still occupied by humans who will not dance in the streets because of their legislative do-goodery. Which is the point of the left-wing douchebag...they believe that the social conscience of the country should be governed by the top down, by buraeucratic intellectual elitists. They beieve in touting 'tolerance' when they really mean 'acceptance'. The former being a state of mind where you may not agree with something, but you'll put up with it, the latter meaning that you had better not say a damn thing about not agreeing with it or face the penalty of becoming a social pariah. The liberal douchebag will often speak of fairness, but really mean that those who actually do something should fork it over to those who don't do shit. They are promoters of doctrines of caring for one one another, as long as it is someone else carries the financial burden and it doesn't affect them. They are the knights of the politicaly correct round table until it gets to the point where they themselves lose out to it and then turn into the self-centered jerks they were all along. The government is their favorite thing, the big tit that will soothe society's problems when in fact it just makes more problems. Douchebag liberals like more government control in a way that a lazy and unorganized person likes direction. They feel that legislating morality is their right and that society is too stupid and backward to handle their lives on their own.

The polical douchebag: This type of douchebag is found on both sides of any aisle. They are the politicians who come into the game simply to line their own pockets and will say whatever is needed at the moment to get it, regardless of what they said in the last moment (to them, that doesn't count...it was the last moment). These are the douchebags who crave power. The ones who need to be 'in charge' as long as being in charge doesn't come with responsibility–which is the dread of any political douchebag. To the polical douchebag, what is wrong is always someone else's fault and the goal of their lives is not to do what is right for the people, but to stay in office as long as possible.

The entertainer douchebag: This type of douchebag goes without saying. They live in a fraudulent on-screen persona that they feverishly cling to, while back in 'reality land' the facts come out. Just like their political counterparts, the actor douchebag is so enamored with his own self-projected persona that he feels he can do whatever he wishes without reprisals. Take Mel Gibson and especially Arnold Schwarzenegger for a couple of examples. Arnold's *60 Minutes* interview about his marital infidelity was a true example of a douchebag who shows no remorse for fucking over his loved ones in the name of instant gratification by getting a little action on the side. Kanye West is another shinning example who only needs about five minutes of airtime to let his douchebaginess shine.

Even more fun is the smugness of these individuals with their causes and their celebrations of themselves as a group. How many award shows are there for the entertainment industry now? If you're a douchebag entertainer, probably not enough because the circle-jerk should never end.

The wealthy douchebag: Having money does not make someone a douchebag, but it helps…a lot. This would be the quintessential douchebag that most of us think about. A wealthy, pompous individual who sees the world through the lens of wealth itself. The reason for this is there is nothing inside the douchebag. The money and its trappings are all he has to convince others that there is life inside of him. The worst sort of moneyed douchebags are that particular case where they know they have not really earned it. This creates an atmosphere of insecurity in the douchebag, predicated on the fear that someone might find out that they have all that money and haven't done a thing to earn it. They are the lottery winners from birth who know that without the money they are really nothing, and that fear comes to them in the night when all is quiet and the money cannot buy them the peace of mind they so desperately need – only Xanax. The other kind of moneyed douchebag is the sort that has gotten his riches from not-quite-honest dealings. This kind is always on the defensive, dreading the moment when their scam of legitimacy is brought out into the sun and exposed for what it is. These can also be dangerous douchebags, because the scam to them is their reality now, and anyone trying to wrest it from them may as well as be trying to take their very lives.

The professional athlete douchebag: These are the ones you see making a fool of themselves in interviews where they speak of their own needs over that of the team, the ones who have wasted immeasurable talent by throwing temper tantrums, or by being more dramatic than athletic. These are the ones you watch throw their lives and talents away because they believe the hype they have created for themselves and feel they are above society and the law. No examples here…there are just too many.

The sports fan douchebag: Now these are some fun guys. The sports fan douchebag is that overbearing sort whose life revolves around any sports club or organization. The sports fan douchebag 'lives and breathes' the failures and successes of these entities, denying any reproach that would say to them that they 'take it too seriously'. They have infused themselves into the action, a sort of voyeuristic inclusion to someplace they would never be invited. Being a sports fan is not in itself a bad thing, but the douchebag is not really such a beast. He has allowed himself to emotionally rise and fall with the fates of strangers who have, in reality, no effect on his life. He has made the fortunes of millionaire entertainers the core being of his life. And that is all that sports really are for any fan. Entertainment. But the douchebag sports fan sees it always as an us-or-them moment. If the team loses, they have lost. They take personally something that has absolutely nothing to do with them. And those around them will suffer.

The gay douchebag: Being gay, that is, being sexually attracted to those of the same sex is nothing new in the world, and most gay people see their proclivity to this as an ad-endum to their humanity. They are human beings who happen to be gay. Not the gay douchebag. Like his heterosexual counterpart 'the playa', the gay douchebag sees his sexual life as the cornerstone of his existence. Like all douchebags, they will be more dramatic, bombastic and overtly push their need for acceptance, bypassing the tolerance issue altogether. The gay douchebag wants to shove their sexuality to the forefront, and like any other douchebag, it is done for the shock value of the act and nothing more. They create attention for themselves by the overt expression of their sexuality, leaving the commonality of shared humanity behind.

The anti-gay douchebag: Then, on the other side of the coin… we have the anti-gay douchebag. These are the folks born of fear and ignorance and hate. To them, anything different from themselves is wrong and must be be punished. The anti-gay douchebag calls on his anger at every turn. In his mind he wants to stamp out a sexual orientation that has been around as long as the oldest profession. Like all douchebags, the anti-gay douchebag acts upon his emotional fears, with no regard for reason and less for tolerance. Probably the greatest of those emotional fears is the fear that gay people dress better than they do.

The religious douchebag: Nothing exemplifies the religious douchebag better than the Westboro Baptist church in the early 21st century. These fun guys are the archetyipcal religious douchebags along the lines of the Spanish Inquisition. To them God is a mean, hateful, pissed off son-of-a-bitch who is gonna send just about everyone to hell unless they adhere to a Christian Talibanesque dogma that they themselves have created. They exemplify, by their public grandstanding, the douchebag's need for attention and the douchebag's insecurity and fear exemplified by anger. It does give one a moment of pause to think that maybe there are more closeted pillow biters in this group than they would like to admit.

Beyond the shining example of the W.B.C. is your ordinary, run-of-the-mill religious douchebag. This is a person who expresses profound faith, love of God, mastery of scripture, and smugness in those things that is seemingly boundless. The one thing the religious douchebag lacks is the practice of his faith outside of the place of worship. Outside of church they are the gossipy, back-stabbing, all-about-me jerk-offs who epitomize being a douchebag. As always, the douchebag has many faces and the religious douchebag has his face for God, but he feels most others are beneath him.

The Atheist douchebag: The athiest douchebag is really the same thing as the religious douchebag, only differing in dogma. They are the quintessential douchebags who, unlike most atheists who simply do not believe in a God, need others to join them and preach a faith much the same as the apostles did. Like all douchebags, they need attention for their belief. They probably need attention for everything in their lives. They try to gain converts at every turn, and like the standard douchebag, have a simmering anger just under the surface that is waiting to come out like a ripe and ready-to-pop zit.

The racist douchebag: Your typical racists are usually individuals so afraid of anything that doesn't remind them of themselves that they succumb to the primitive need to lash out at anyone who doesn't fit their idea of what people should look like. As with any douchebag, it's their fear and insecurity that rules their thought process. A need to feel superior while wandering the bleak and barren landscape of their own souls. These are the special kind of jerk-offs who hurl the human race backwards a few thousand years. With no real or clear understanding that human beings of every race offer something to this world, they have a need to make a competition of skin color and physical features. It's the idiot's way of getting a hand up by putting down others who look different without any regard for their true nature.

The pushy douchebag: Pushy douchebags are the overbearing individuals who demand action from others to support their ideas of what the world should be. These are the 'I want what I want' kind of assholes who expect others to meet whatever fucked-up idea they have about how things should be. They are the complainers who, when pressed for a logical or reasonable explanation for their grievance, can only come up with a feeble emotional tirade reminding all around them that they are still the spoiled little child who needs a spanking.

The Salesperson douchebag: Salesperson douchebags have only one thing in mind…to line their own pockets. A normal salesperson understands the value of customer service and the importance of building positive relationships with those they serve. Douchebag salespersons are the modern day snake-oil salesmen. They endeavor to make a quick hit and get the hell out of town. The quality of whatever they sell means very little to them, and reasonable complaints do not factor into their reasoning. Just like other douchebags, they work quickly because they know the longer they expose themselves to a possible mark, the more they will look like the dickhead that they truly are.

The senior citizen douchebag: They are the standard bearers of the 'Golden years', the champions of social security and the complainers about the government. They have long outlasted their turn at being productive in society and now focus their attention of all things from the viewpoint of being somehow cheated of their youth. They resist the simple fact that aging is a part of life and, well yes, things are going to change for them. Senior douchebags are people who most likely were douchebags in their youth, and now in the twilight of advancing age, they go full bore. They are the soul suckers who look with a jealous eye at those who still have the vigor that they feel has been robbed from them. They demand discounts for their age, special services for their handicaps, someone to listen to the endless, depressing stories of doctor visits, procedures, and who's dead today. They are the assholes who didn't prepare financially for the future and now consider that to be someone else's problem. The only thing they bring to the table is insatiable neediness that would make most vibrant seniors cringe.

The environmentalist Douchebag: These are not the folks who endeavor to live their lives without creating too much waste or quietly do the small things that help to make our world a little bit nicer than it was before. The douchebags of this particular bent are the outraged assholes who desire to cause a scene at every turn in their never-ending crusade to rid the world of anything they see as a detriment to it.

Geroge Carlin said it best:

> "…the greatest arrogance of all is 'save the planet'. Are these fucking people kidding me? Save the planet? We don't even know how to take care of ourselves yet, we haven't learned to care for one another and we're going to save the fucking planet?"

Once again this particular douchebag is discernable by their outrage, a classic douchebag maneuver that seeks to create drama around an abstract idea. For any douchebag, the drama they create makes the conversation more real. And as with all douchebags, it is a bluster of no significance and changes nothing: it only gives the douchebag an emotional outlet to release pent-up anxiety or aggression on some unexpecting poor bastard who just wanted to eat his lunch that happened to be served on a Styrofoam plate and is now being accused of destroying the planet because he was hungry.

Douchebag teachers: Most teachers understand that their job is to teach their students material that will benefit the student in the future and help them make good decisions in the present or simply to help the student learn a trade or skill. Not so for the douchebag teacher. Their job, they have have decided, is not to teach students *how* to think critically, but rather *what* to think. Douchebag teachers somehow, in the vast reaches of their insecure minds decide that how they *feel* about certain things is so important (they're douchebags; everything they think is important) that they need to indoctrinate their students into seeing things their way. The epitome of the teaching douchebag, however, is the one who not only seeks to indoctrinate their students in their way of thinking, but also, in true douchebag fashion, make up the facts as they go to support their argument, leaving the children completely fucked when they need to deal with concrete issues that actually affect their lives and the lives of others around them.

8

The Douchebag Genome Project

An Entirely Unscientific Scientific Study of Douchebag Genetic Origins.

Some are born to douchebaggery, and others have douchebaggery thust upon them.

Being a blithering asshole is a condition that some people aspire to their entire lives. From birth to the calling of the grave, these people tend to drag everyone they come in contact with into their morass of neediness, into an abyss of misery that the douchebag reins over like a dark lord of bullshit. How do people become like this? What are the origins? Were they born that way? Why are lamb chops so delicious? These and other questions will be answered here.

Fight or Flight: There are different forms of intelligence in the universe. Some are innate, and some are learned. The innate intellligence, for example, is how newborn mammals can, without any training, find momma's tit and know exactly what to do with it. It's survival on a basic scale. The same sort of intelligence works when we sleep. In that state, our consciousness is lowered but our hearts still beat and lungs still breathe (some breathe much more loudly than others, but that's not the point), keeping our bodies going. As the body grows, so also does the mind, taking in what it sees around it, trying to process it into need or want, and moving onto the next. In children, this can be exemplified by a toy.

In a child's mind a toy is an absolute embodiment of their selves and when separated from it, they have the possibility of throwing a holy shit storm. Return the toy and they are placid again, playing with it until they move on to the next item of interest. In the basic context, this is the flight or fight instinct which is innate and will develop in its complexity as the life of the child also grows in complexity. The child here fights with the only weapon he has…emotional trauma. His temper tantrum is the weapon that is two fold. One, he gets attention for his needs, and two, he gets the object of his desire—the toy—returned to him. Another example is two children playing with separate toys where the first child sees the second as having more fun than he, and thus he goes over, thumps child two on the head and takes the toy for himself, believing he will also get the pleasure of play that child two possesed while child two goes into the aforementioned hissy fit.

This kind of behavior can be evident in adults also, which is why you're reading this. Some douchebags are born that way, live their lives that way and never seem to grow out of it. The phrase 'you can't grow a conscience' applies to them and is one of the reason why we have such a girth of laws involving human actions in the world. The child wants his toy, and he'll do whatever he needs to get it. The only thing that changes is the nature of the toy and the means of aquisition. As the child gets older the toys turn into power and control for varying reasons of insecurity, and the child's hissy fit turns into anger and eventually aggression and violence. Even though the toys change, and the manner of acquisition changes, the basic premise remains. Some asshole wants what he wants, develops a sense of entitlement to it and then fights to get it. The flight instinct kicks in usually when the asshole gets caught trying to get something that he has no legal entitlement to.

Nature vs. Nurture

The nature douchebag: As douchebags grow older the form of the 'toy' becomes more complex and the nature of the 'fight' does also. The sandbox transforms into the social world or the board room but the insecurities remain the same. The nature of the conflict changes but the source remains the same. The adult douchebag doesn't know the difference in an emotional way. He may now be fighting not for a toy, but for a superficial reputation that he never possessed. He will need to enforce that illusion, and he'll do it with a fight, until an overwhelming force of reality and facts will force him to give up the fight.

This is a typical scenario on the politcal stage that can be seen at least weekly. Being a douchebag can be complex, but the one thing that stands out always is the need for the douchebag to retain his 'image' even if in the process of retaining that image, he in essence destroys it. This 'genetic douchebag' is predisposed throughout his life to get things to build up his fragile sense of self esteem; be it money, power, sex, or property, the underlying goal is control, and he will be constantly in need of more, no matter how much he gets. In the end it is that need which destroys him, either by financial ruin, a nice extended stay in a state-run facility, or by alienating everyone who comes into his life.

The nurture douchebag: These are the douchebags who learned their craft at the foot of some master in their lives. These mentors of douchebaggery are simply passing the torch of selfishness and hate onto the next generation, weaving their need for control into the conscious fabric of the young. These are the parents who want their children to follow in their own footsteps, or the parent who wants their children to fulfill some long unattained goal that they failed to attain. These are the douchebag parents who want only their own satisfaction, and not the child's. In addition to that there are the parents who train their children to react to every setback with rage and anger. They do this by the example of, well, reacting to every setback with rage and anger. They themselves never developed past this point in their stunted development, so why should their children? There are also the douchebag teachers and coaches whose need to indoctrinate rather than foster thinking is their idea of teaching and instilling in young athletes not the idea of reaching inside and doing your personal best, but rather, finding something or someone to complete against as a measure of self-worth. And so it goes, the cycle continuing forever, creating douchebags for all seasons.

9

The Douchebag Industrial Complex

"Advertising has us chasing cars and clothes, working jobs we hate so we can buy shit we don't need."
"Sticking feathers up your butt doesn't make you a chicken."
"We are consumers. We're the byproducts of a lifestyle obsession."

Tyler Durden, *Fight Club,*
-Chuck Palahniuk

Advertising: Being a douchebag is being in a state of prepetual arrested development, and is the antithesis of any kind spiritual growth with a rigid superficial and selfish view of life and the world. To be a douchebag is to forever be needy for something.

This is a great market to sell shit to.

For those who sell things, the age group that can roughly be defined by the ages between fifteen and thirty are prime targets. As a generalization, people in that age range tend to impulse purchase more, tend to make purchases based on a need to superficially attain a social standing or the need to maintain a social standing. They are more easily manipulated by sexual perceptions and the desire to buy items to enhance their perceived sexual prowess. Although the ability to manipulate this group makes them a prime target for marketers, it is limited. So what the ad-men try to do is to extend that range, sell youth as the ultimate and only state to be in, and sell products that will help keep you young long after nature says it is time to give it up. Keeping people in a perpetual state of mid-life crisis insures a greater market of not-quite-informed and not-quite-thinking individuals whose needs can be created at will and who can be sold products to fulfill the artificially-created need.

We all need things in this world. Food, water, clothing, shelter. These are the basics, and there are those who manufacure and sell these items in a modern society. The item itself makes no difference; what does seem to make a difference is the perception. Advertisers do not, in most cases, want people to think of the true nature of what they are selling; they want you to think of the way it will make you feel about yourself. If you notice in stores that there are items strategically placed so that younger children will have them at eye level it is because children have a greater sense of attachment to things and can be more easily manipulated to be the catalyst for a sale. Mom will invariably buy the thing of interest to the child if it will shut him up.

Douchebag adults are the same way, but the things they want to buy cost a lot more, so advertisers need to make the return much more profound. This is especially true in the automotive industry. How often do advertisers pitch some abstract (non-existent) aspect of a vehicle rather than its true attributes? How often do they place a vehicle in some impossible location to emphasize its glamour, or make it seem that the vehicle can do the impossible? Often, it seems, but why?

The truth is that the advertisers are not selling a product, but rather, they are selling an illusion of how that product will transform you into someone you want to be. Do you want to be a rugged outdoorsy individualist? Buy a Jeep to drive in the urban jungles. Got more money than sense? Then get a Hummer. Need a vehicle to make others believe you are very successful? Buy a fast, glamourous, two-door payment plan that maybe you can't afford. The same goes for clothing and other personal items. The idea is not to sell you a thing, but rather to sell you the illusion of fulfillment that possessing that thing will give you. Douchebags cling to the social aspect of items, just the way teenagers do with fashion. Why? Because douchebags are little more than emotional teenagers who desire to be viewed as something they wish to be, whether they are or not. It's the douchebag's image that is at stake, and Madison Avenue will be happy to show you the way to the perfect you that you never will be. A douchebag paradise of false impression to get the attention for who they *want* to be. An ongoing revolving door of products to make the 65-year old grandfather as sexually vibrant as he was at 16. Makeup to transform the 65 year-old grandmother to look like a 65 year-old grandmother with too much make-up but to her it makes her look 30. It says so on the box.

For advertisers and the products they represent, the target object is nothing more than fear. Fear is the ultimate mover and shaker. Whether it is the fear of not being who you think you should be, or the univerasal fear of getting older and death, they have a product for you. And in the absence of fear, they are the masters of creating it, along with that 'new and improved' magic thing that will create the ultimate illusion of safety.

News: Along with advertisers, most news outlets understand that fear is the best seller. Fear to the douchebag is the clarion call to action. And to a douchebag the action is simply a continuous blathering of words about how this crisis or that crisis is going to destroy whatever and wherever. The truth about the news is that it never really changes. With a few detail modifications a newspaper from the 1800's would read very much like one from today. A truthful headline in the paper could be this: "Stupid people did some stupid shit to some other people today, instigating the other people to do some stupid shit in response."

Broadcast news is even more fun. These guys sometimes don't even let the facts of a story get in the way of entertainment or fear mongering. They are selective as to what they like to broadcast (inflammatory and negative stories are the best), while sometimes even changing facts and real outcomes to fit perceptions. Exploding gas tanks come to mind here, as well as many other examples. In a world filled with whackos and weird shit, they somehow feel the need to lower the bar and their credibility along with it. But the truth remains that as long as there are people, there will be people behaving badly, acting out inappropriately, emotionally or self-servingly to the point where they fuck shit up for themselves and everyone else. Broadcast news is the chronicle of the douchebag culture, or rather the cronicle of the douchebag culture brought to you by douchebags themselves.

Reality T.V.: For douchebags, being on T.V. is the ultimate ego trip. People watch them, recognize them on the street, seek autographs, and treat them like the stars they have always wanted to be. But these douchebags know somewhere inside that they are not famous for something; rather, they are famous for being famous. Producers know that by casting douchebags in their programs they will be creating drama. Drama entertains the audiences. The greater the audience, the greater the advertising revenues. So, if this were a logic equation, then more douchebags on T.V. equates to more money for producers. The number of self-absorbed douchebags on T.V. in the early 21st century proves that fact.

Putting a douchebag on T.V. and encouraging them to be the biggest asshole they can be is good for laughs. But more often than not the douchebag and his dickhead ways seem to prevail. From *Survivor* to *Swamp People*, they give audiences the illusion that a life without drama is no life at all, creating a new generation of humans who proceed to recreate the realm of this unreal reality in their own lives, making douchebags of themselves and being a royal pain in the ass to most others who they come in contact with. The reality T.V. culture nurtures the douchebag in people and announces to the world that if you're an asshole, you'll get publicity...the ultimate attention.

10

I, Docuhebag

The Duochebag in Us All, and How to Minimize It

"We have met the enemy and he is us."

-Walt Kelly

"Emancipate yourself from mental slavery; none but ourselves can free our minds."

Redemption Song
-Bob Marley

"The only thing necessary for the triumph of evil is for good men to do nothing"

-Edmund Burke

Everyone has a little douchebag in them. Everyone has moments in their lives that they wish they could take back, do over, or make right. There are times when our mouths run out of control before our brains can catch up, moments when our actions are more self-serving than of service, situations where our taking is not limited to what is ours to take. It is part of the human condition, but not being aware of it has consequences.

Under stress and anxiety our selfish nature comes out, and our actions are dictated not by rational thinking, but by emotional excess. Using emotions to solve problems is much like using a hammer to paint a wall – wrong tool for the wrong job. Have you ever heard of someone describing another's actions as "well, he really fucked up because he was thinking calmly and rationally and with consideration for others?" Doesn't happen.

A full-fledged douchebag *habitually* does selfish and thoughtless things more often than not, whereas for most people it is an occasional and momentary lapse of reason. Things happen in life that create emotional stress (be the stress real or imagined) and can cause us to react with even more emotion, but usually we work through the emotion to a point of calm where, with more wisdom in hand, we make better decisions. We've all had moments of afterthought where the clarion call to the self is 'what the hell was I thinking?' The truth is, you were not thinking, you were using primitive emotion to solve a problem that only worsened the problem by the use of that emotion. This is the realm of the douchebags. They see everything (even in the 'need to impress' mode) from the emotional standpoint of getting for the self or maintaining for the self. Other people in the life of a douchebag function only to support this viewpoint. Whether it be a material thing, mental thing or emotional thing, the douchebag wants to either get it, or keep it, and if you get in his way, you are seen as a threat to the illusion of his very self, which to a douchebag *is* the reality of himself. The more people become lost in illusions the more douchebaggy they become.

How to minimize the douchebag inside: The fact is that we all have the douchebag gene in us. It is a primitave survival instinct carried over from the hunter-gatherers that we were at the emergence of the human race. Being a douchebag then meant you survived another day, and in the period of early humanity, short time was the *only* time. Even though the philosophy of 'live like there is no tomorrow' is the off-shoot of this mental pre-programming, the truth of the matter is that more often than not, there is a tomorrow, and the words and actions of today will have an impact on them. Another great saying is 'it's better to burn up than fade away', but most of those looking to do so wind up only 'burning out' and simply become a burden on the rest of society.

Lessening the douchebag inside requires a mind-set that can be almost impossible for some to grasp (douchebags can't; that's why they're the real thing). It requires the suspension of the illusion of 'self'. The illusion of self is the 'bubble of bullshit' that we sometimes encase ourselves in. It is the story of ourselves that we want others to believe. It is, as a modern example, Lance Armstrong, creating his own bubble of bullshit that he vigorously defended in courts of law and on a personal level that destroyed others around him. We all have such a bubble, but true douchebags have bubbles that are fucking huge and they defend them vigorously, sometimes with rage and violence. Most people have a small bubble that collapses under the weight of our own reason and common sense. Being a real douchebag is to support, maintain, vigorously defend, and if possible grow the bubble despite facts and realities to the contrary. Getting rid of the bubble is the process of seeing things from the perspective of reality and the realm of eternity. Not easy shit to think about sometimes. But the fact of the matter is that everything we have changes and transforms or goes away. Period. Truth. So don't look at the things you have gathered around you as the truth of you. Those things will change, they will transform, or they will go away.

Attachment to things is the first mental construct that should be flushed down the golden toilet. Those things are not you. The job you have doesn't define you. It is something you do, and the more attachment you have to it as an identity, then the greater the bubble, and the greater the fall when it pops, as it will, eventually. The illusion that you cannot live without someone else is another bubble that will eventually pop. It's an illusion that your attachment to someone defines who you are, and this lessens the relationship with that person, because with that attachment comes insecurity and in some cases, the tragic outcome of 'if I can't have him or her, no one will'. This is where the attachment goes horribly wrong, and shows only a selfish neediness that has nothing to do with love.

Letting go of attachments does not at all mean that you cannot have appreciation for people and things; in fact it strengthens that appreciation. This is something a douchebag cannot do. The douchebag needs to control or possess the objects of his appreciation because his mental makeup transforms the appreciation into a desire. The desire emotion reminds the douchebag that he is lacking in something or that someone else has something that would add to his bubble of himself—his illusion of himself, and so he lacks the ability to appreciate things unless he owns them in some way, or these things enhance him personally. If the douchebag cannot possess these things, he will most likely verbally put them down to others or dismiss them. His not possessing them, in his mind, is grounds to dismiss them. The same goes for positive events in the lives of others or the possessions of others that do not enhance him.

Overcoming this douchebag nature in ourselves can be done rather easily even if you have to do it from a mental construct at first. Simply make a verbal appreciation of things or people or situations, giving credit where it's due. This will develop a sense of detachment from possession and value. In other words, if you appreciate things of others without having to possess them, be it character, accomplishment, actions, or physical possessions, you will lessen the ego's desire to require them to be *your* possessions to be of value. This is the antithesis of the 'keeping up with the Jones" mentality. Eventually it will eliminate the douchebag mantra of jealousy and envy and will set you free to appreciate what you *do* have in your life.

Get real with what you really need as opposed to what you want: Understanding the difference between these two can keep asshole actions to a minimum. A need is something that will maintain you, as a living person. If we honestly boil down our needs we will eventually come up with a very short list of possessions that are truly necessary and activities that we truly desire to participate in. The typical douchbag doesn't have the ability to do this; his mind is programmed for excess of some sort, always needing more. The need is an illusion and not reality, but it's impossible for a douchebag to see the differnce. His wants are his desires, and he feels less if he is not chasing his desires. Like a child, he will do what he has to do to get them before moving on to some other desire. What he doesn't see is that his desire is an acknowledgment of lacking in himself. How can someone desire something unless he sees himself as lacking it? It's impossible. Unless someone is batshit crazy, they don't desire a cheeseburger when a cheeseburger is right in front of them. If we add this to the 'Douchebag industrial complex' we have a great carrot-and-stick scenario that defines social living in the modern world.

Lessening our wants and clarifying our needs does not mean we have to live like monks. Not at all, but what it can do for you is to set you free from superficial desires that only serve a short-term outcome (remember the child and his toy). Take a look around your home sometime and you'll see some of the things there that do not have a purpose in your life, things that you have worked hard for the money to acquire or have gone into debt to obtain. Somewhere along the line you let yourself be convinced that you needed it, but after a short period that need went away, and there you are staring at that 'scramble the egg in the shell' machine. We've all done it.

Don't let it bring you down, because when you bought that thing, a strong and powerful force was leading you toward that decision, one that you were not even aware of. But now you know, so next time don't 'pick up the phone right now' and wait a while. Once the douchebag industrial complex's pointed assault on your common sense has abated, the impulse to buy will also abate. Realize that the things that will have true value in your life will *always* have value and after a period of time it will either be apparent or it will fade away.

Lessen your desire to express your opinions: This requires mental training; self-discipline, and especially, self-control. Douchebags have a loathing for both of those things, or simply cannot comprehend them.

Everyone has opinions about certain things. But the truth of the matter is that our opinions are usually a knee-jerk reaction to partial information, or, especially for a douchebag, an expression of his own true nature. The douchebag lives for this. His knee-jerk reactions to him are an expression of his knowledge of the world around him, and nine out of ten times, the douchebag doesn't have a fucking clue about what he's talking about. He's simply trying to look good, and his ignorant judgment at the time reflects his weak perception skills. The problem is that his perceptions have no value of empathy, or consideration of the perspective of others. What the douchebag does is define a thing, situation or person in relation to his own thinking. For a douchebag, others are only extensions of himself, and everyone thinks the way he does; therefore whatever is, or is happening, will be defined by his own nature.

Letting go of this form of douchebaggery frees you to see things as they are. The need for knee-jerk reactions lessens as your instinctual mind tells you there is no need to define things, and at the very least no need to define things instantly. The fact of the matter is that your judging or defining anything has no impact on that thing whatsoever. Your judgment only defines you. When you practice this you see that *not* expressing instant opinions gives you time to truly evaluate what is going on.

Avoid comparisons: One of the hardest things for a douchebag not to do is compare themselves to others. A douchebag has little or nothing inside and therefore has to find his worth with positive comparisons of himself to others. To him it defines reality. He desires to look better than someone else and that satiates his desire for self-value.

When we do this, it can limit us to what others are or have done. It can create a status-quo that, once achieved or overcome, stops us there. We've proven to ourselves we are better than someone else. But have we really done the best we can do? Or did we stop when we passed someone else who we were comparing ourselves to?

Limiting ourselves this way deprives us of our ability 'to be' and replaces it with the limits of being better than someone else. It is a typical predicament in a regimented society and holds back individuals from doing their very best.

Reduce the habit of emotional over-reaction: There are times and circumstances where emotions are necessary, appropriate and cathartic. But they can, when used too much, become a bad habit that makes others run from your sight like a scalded ape. Everyone knows someone who is that person who you just don't tell things to because you know that person is going to throw a conniption fit. The fit is a knee-jerk reaction that has been self-trained into that individual, either by emulating someone else or by trial and error. He does so out of fear (the fear of being harmed by something) and typically the fear is some form of harm to that person's ego or sense of self. Emotional reactions are something that those who excessively express them will defend as a right. They also tend to accuse those who do not sympathize with them of having no feelings. Typically the emotional outrage or hurt feelings are based on some trivial thing or occurrence, taken out of context or simply not understood. But the reaction will be dramatic, and the reason a douchebag does it is to regain control of some situation or to regain their own sense of self that they feel has been damaged or marred in some way.

Those who seem to always be on the verge of rage or on the verge of tears are letting others know that they are fragile, small people who posses no real sense of themselves or of the reality of the world around them. When they are not faced with some small thing to get upset about, they will ussually create something out of thin air, just like a jerk-off magician.

The way *not* to do this is by creating the habit of trying to be conscious in all situations. The douchebag gene that resides in us all does not have an appreciation for consciousness. The douchebag gene wants to rant, to rage, to be offended by as much as it possibly fucking can. If left unchecked it will always find something to be outraged about. But by being consciously present and inhibiting the douchebag gene, it will eventually have less of an impact on you. It will never go away, but like any other fear, the more exposure to reality (in this case the absurdity of emotional reactions when they clearly are not called for), the less of an impact these emotions will have and the less close to the surface they will be.

A good example of this is how a fear of water reacts to swimming lessons. Fear of water cannot exist unless you consciously allow it to exist by not going in the water. By getting in the water and eventually learning to swim, the fear of water will not go away but it will be diminished to an inconsequential thought that has been squashed by the continuous reality of you swimming in water.

Fear is something that exists because it is a basic survival instinct. It exists to keep us from some harm, real or perceived. For a douchebag, fear is a constant thing because their existence revolves around a false sense of themselves and is at constant risk of being exposed as false and therefore 'killed'. Nothing is more fragile than something that exists only in the imagination. To keep this bullshit at bay in yourself can only come about by facing the facts as they stand and *not* taking every situation in life personally. For a douchebag, this is nearly impossible. Everything that happens has something to do with them, because they see themselves as the center of the universe.

Practice empathy: Empathy is the ability to see things from the *perspective* of someone else. It differs from sympathy in that sympathy denotes agreement with a sentiment whereas empathy denotes understanding. Empathy is a quality that your average douchebag does not possess. The douchebag sees things from his own point of view only; even his *attempts* at seeing things from another's point of view is skewed. Other points of view to a douchebag are simply his point of view put into a different situation. And since the douchebag's point of view is the only possible reality, then others, if they are thinking right, should also have the same view.

A true sense of empathy begins when you start out with the three most intelligent words you will ever speak, and they are –'I don't know'. A douchebag can have a very tough time with that phrase. They simply can't be without an answer and will, more often than not, substitute their opinion for a fact of some point. To a douchebag it's all the same anyway, their opinions being simply the very best thinking possible on the earth.

Practicing 'I don't know' begins with yourself first and foremost. You don't have to go around mumbling it at every turn, but get into the habit of telling it to yourself before the douchebag gene rushes up to the front of the class with some bullshit, fabricated story that will make drama happen. Once you can master 'I don't know', you can move on to next step of 'I'll find out'. You will notice that when you can truthfully tell yourself and others that you don't know—when you don't—then the shit you wanted to define in a knee-jerk reactionary way doesn't really matter, and you'll want to find out less about that shit (and eventually you'll come to the startling realization that most of the shit you thought you knew about, and you didn't, really was shit that didn't matter in the first place).

Practicing 'I don't know' will sometime be difficult, especially when confronted by douchebags who *need* you to know. Just realize that their need is not yours. If needing to know is not your job, if you're breathing, have eaten recently, and have a roof over your heard, just simply make a mental note for those folks to go fuck themselves, smile and walk away.

Realize it's not about you: Human ego, when allowed to ripen too much, will spoil. When that happens an individual will most likely personalize everything around them, whether they are involved in something or not. They take negative events and construct an egotistical buttress to keep themselves from emotional harm. They fall into the unconscious habit of defending themselves, their perspectives, and their actions simply because their thought process is grounded in superficial appearance, which is the overriding sense of self for a douchebag.

Having a reality-based perspective of yourself will allow you to perform at your personal best while minimizing the uninformed opinions of others.

Remember that many times, especially with douchebags, the opinions expressed by them is simply projection. In other words, they will define things and people not by inquiring into the true nature of what they observe, but rather by what *they* would be thinking or doing in the place of the other person in the situation. A douchebag doesn't have a very good sense of empathy, thus they cannot really understand the thoughts or opinions of others even when they are expressed clearly to them. When you take the expressions of others personally, you are allowing others to control your thoughts, anger you, make you defensive and less sure of yourself and the things you do. You have unwittingly allowed them to be, at least temporarily, in control of you, and like any puppet, it will become a habit that will have you more like a pinball in a machine than a person focused on doing their best.

By always striving to consciously do the best you can at whatever you are doing, you take away the impact of the opinions of others simply because *you know* you're doing the best you can. The negative opinions of others become irrelevant in the face of that fact. The problem again is that we often do not do our best because we are distracted by what we perceive others will think of us.

Consciously doing your best also eliminates the need for comparison with others and allows you to appreciate the skills of others. The opposite is either a personally limiting comparison of yourself with others (i.e. when you strive to do better than someone else, you strive less when you have surpassed that person). This is one of the negatives to promoting competition…human nature tends to play down to the level of a rival.

Work to eliminate snap judgments from your thinking: The power of 'I don't know' expressed in silence to yourself will help keep the inner douchebag in you at bay. Douchebags do not have this ability. Their daily lives are a constant series of fast, information-lacking decisions based on emotional rationalization that serves no one but their false sense of themselves. Unless there is an immediate need for decision making, for example, an emergency situation, the need for quick decisions is wholly without merit. Start with 'I don't know', and if you truly find that you wish to know more then follow it up with, 'I'm going to find out'. The douchebag doesn't have this ability; they have already judged a situation, and will either gloat in their prediction being right, or will be faced with the need to justify it if wrong, usually at the expense of another. Most of the time you will find that 'I don't know' spoken to yourself will be enough and that 'I will find out' doesn't come along simply because you're grounding yourself in a reality that makes you realize that knowing stupid, silly shit doesn't fucking matter.

11

The Agenda of the Douchebag

Dealing with douchebags can be an arduous task, especially in the realm of communication. It is there that the douchebag's gift for subterfuge and twisting of facts becomes apparent. What the douchebag hears and what they say often have little to do with what is really being discussed. It can be absolutely confusing and even frightening trying to figure out what's going on with them. Trying to keep things on an even keel can be near impossible, and trying to figure out the truth can be even more so.

For the douchebag, every encounter, every conversation, every human interaction is a desperate and anxious attempt to validate the false self they have created to represent themselves, or an opportunity to build up that false self. To that end, everyone the douchebag encounters has a role to play, and that role is to support the douchebag's false ideas. Your presence is to serve that twisted master, and once again, your cooperation in the matter doesn't have to be voluntary. In their presence, if you are not supportive (hell, even if you are), the douchebag will find the need to put down you or the things you do. This helps the douchebag elevate himself in his mind without actually having to do anything.

When the douchebag doesn't have the social room to do this overtly, they usually resort to a more subtle form of putdown. It typically revolves around a mild compliment that is followed up by a much more potent insult. What the douchebag is trying to do is reinforce his ego, and that of course means a sacrifice of others, since the douchebag doesn't really need to make improvements to himself. A few examples are as follows:

YOU: "Hey, I'm going to do 'xyz' tomorrow."

DOUCHEBAG: "You don't know anything about 'xyz'", or, "you're not very good at 'xyz'. Why would you want to do that?"

What the douchebag is saying is a form of resentment, jealousy or insecurity and your participation in that activity doesn't make him look good in the instant you tell him. The more subtle approach, when the douchebag feels he is not in complete control of the relationship, would be something like this:

YOU: "Hey, I'm going to do 'xyz' tommorow."

DOUCHEBAG: "Yeah, that's great. I used to do 'xyz', but after I mastered it, it just became boring, and I'm above that now."

In the first example the douchebag's put down is overt. He has put you down directly. In the second example, he is elevating himself above you indirectly, expressing his aloofness in the matter. Depending on what kind of feedback the douchebag has gotten in the period prior to you talking to him will determine the response. If the douchebag is having a very bad day, he may react to your statement of intent with outright anger.

In either case, what the douchebag hears and then says has very little to do with what was actually said. The douchebag mind is sort of a blender on constant puree. He may or may not hear what you are saying, but he almost always pushes the puree button to make himself look and temporarily feel better about himself. The only time he may choose not to do so is if there is an audience around who might call him on his bullshit or simply see it as a jerk-off response. In those cases he is in the 'need to impress' mode, and that will not permit him to indulge his thoughts of a knee-jerk response. But be assured those thoughts are there, waiting for the opportunity to come out.

The douchebag mind is very adept at defining things in an instant. Like our media, they want to be the first to speak out about any subject, to define it, pigeonhole it or insist on the real nature of anything. Question them at your own peril. Disprove them with even more peril. They do not see it as being wrong about their definitions but rather as you making them look bad.

One predominant factor that can be said about the douchebag is that the more you find yourself in the company of them, the more you will eventually become like them. This happens when you realize the only way to defend yourself against them is to battle them on their ground, using anger, deceit, insults, irrational judgments, and put-downs. Then eventually it will no longer be a defense against just douchebags, you will do these things to everyone, and you will have become a full fledged member of a dubious group of assholes, perpetuating the way of the jerk-off.

12

Ridding Yourself of a Douchebag

A douchebag is a tedious pain in the ass. You never know when the other shoe will drop, and most likely, it will be a shoe you had no idea existed. Their very nature lends itself to minimizing your presence, your needs, and in essence, minimizing you as a human being except at those times when you are needed, then the charm comes on...sometimes. Before you come to the conclusion that you *need* to continue to deal with a douchebag, you need to ask a few tough questions of yourself and also sweep away a few illusions.

The first question is the essential one. It is simple in nature but more complex emotionally and socially.

Do you need to keep this asshole in your life?

In other words, do you need to keep putting up with strange, self-absorbed bullshit, day in and day out? The best way to answer this question is to make two lists. One will be the benefits of sticking around, and the other the drawbacks. The list is for you alone, so you need to be very honest with yourself, keep the facts straight and the emotional embellishment to a minimum (even if one of the negatives is emotional stress). Once you have your list done, then prioritize it. The best and the worst at the top, followed by the rest. Then look again at the top issues and decide, honestly, which ones mean the most to you.

For example, if you're married and your partner provides you with financial security and you rate that more important than, let's say...the lack of emotional love, then you need to come to the realization that that is your choice. Don't be fooled thinking the situation will change. If you've read through this book, you now know that there is going to be no change, only the situational suggestion of it, never lasting longer that it benefits the douche-bag. So deal with it, make your choices and live with them.

If while comparing the two lists, you realize that the negatives are more important than the positives, then it's time to pack your shit and get yourself out of the belly of the beast.

If the situation is job related, either stay with the resignation that you need the money or get your resume ready and get it out. Do this in absolute discretion. If the douchebag in your life is your boss, chances are good that he or she, once they get wind that you want to leave, will adopt a stance of rejection, or worse, betrayal. These are things a douchebag does on a consistent basis, and feeling betrayed is something a douchebag can't stand no matter how badly they've treated you. They will adopt a pose that you are an ungrateful worker. So keep your intentions under wraps and get the fuck outta there.

If the situation is a personal one, then the decision-making paradigm is going to be tougher, ranging from divorce to distancing a casual acquaintence. If it's a close personal relationship or a marriage and, after you've made your list, you've come to the 'pack your shit and go' conclusion, then you need to start making preparations for your departure.

The worst-case scenario is being married with children. With that kind of break the preparation details need to be exact. You will need to know where you are going, how you are going to live and what's going to happen to the children. The douchebag spouse will react to your leaving them the same way the douchebag boss does, with rejection and a sense of betrayal. Even if it's a philandering husband, he will portray himself as the victim, and in a divorce setting will often go for retribution. This will seem illogical with no basis in reality, but that's probably the reason you're leaving his ass in the first place. He will attempt to align your children against you, since they will be some of the more powerful pawns he has to manipulate. Even attempts at reconciliation will only be another act that he will drop as soon as he gets what he wants. Don't be fooled. Stand your ground and stay the course. Get out, because it will not get better.

For causual acquaintances and friends, it's a bit easier. Just lessen contact with them and eventually they will find someone else to manipulate. Don't make accusations about their behavior or call them on the carpet. Those are things that the douchebag doesn't understand (personal responsibility) and he will see it as an un-provoked attack. His false bubble of himself cannot deal with the reality of his actions, so they are stuffed into a place in his twisted head where he knows they are true, but he doesn't have to deal with them, and he most likely never will.

After a while, after lessening contact, the douchebag will even-tually fade away, his ego repaired as he twists his reasoning into some scenario that makes him look good. There may even be disparaging remarks at your expense, but the reality will be the same…the batshit crazy asshole is no longer in your life, he can-not get back into your life and screw it up because you've simply removed him from it, and he is gone.

If the individual is a close friend, the process can be more un-comfortable, but if you've realized that the person is a douchebag, then you know that betrayal is only another private conversation away, that their loyalty is only to themselves, and what they say means nothing.

13

Surviving the Douchebag Apocalypse

Dealing with a Douchebag—
If You Really, Really Have To

"There are no exceptions. If you choose to dance with the devil, do not expect to lead."

-Anonymous

If you've made your list, and made it truthfully, and you came to the conclusion that you really cannot break away from the situation, then you need to take some steps to lessen the emotional and mental impact of the douchebag you simply can't let go of.

You'll need a game plan and will need to create boundaries and barriers. One trait of the douchebag you can use to your advantage is their lack of empathy. They simply cannot perceive what others are thinking or feeling, even when those thoughts and feelings are explained to them, so you can go about dealing with them while they continue to think that they are in charge. Many of these suggestions will make most people cringe, and indeed, they are a false play that you need to act out in order to keep yourself mentally and emotionally from going off the cliff. It can be difficult and may seem farcical at times, but these suggestions will at the least create a more livable environment for yourself.

Be careful and try not to universalize these tactics with everyone. Some people will see through the display and consider you to be shallow and ingenuine. Remember, these tactics are to help you get through life *dealing with a douchebag*, and not the general population. Not everyone is a flaming asshole and to treat them as such only makes you more the douchebag.

Stroking: Douchebags are very much like small children in grown-up bodies who need to be praised. Their sense of self-esteem is tied closely to the outside world and their inner-core of self is woefully underdeveloped. Their lives are that of a parasitic nature where they move from host to host looking for a reflection of themselves that validates themselves. So give it to them. Give them all the ball-cupping and pussy-rubbing you can stand to put out there without vomiting or laughing yourself silly. The douchebag will most likely have no idea that it is ingenuine, having no clue about how others *really* feel because he doesn't have the capacity to do so. The closest thing he can muster is a vague sense of how he *thinks* others feel about him. So lay it on; it will undoubtedly help to keep the negativity at least to a minimum. The douchebag needs to put others down to feel a sense of a higher self. And those others, if they are close, make the high all that more potent. So make a demonstrative point to put him at ease and let him know how great he is...and try not to laugh.

If the douchebag in your world is a supervisor or boss, it can be tricky. Typically, they are incompetent in some aspect of the job they have, or they are very competent and have an arrogance in regards to it. Either way, like all human beings, they will make mistakes and things will go wrong. No one bats 1000, inevitable and unforeseeable events happens, and humans are fallible (unless you're the Pope, who claims otherwise). It is during these moments of failure (real or perceived) that the douchebag in them comes out. As an employee, your job (in addition to doing your job) will also be to pacify the douchebag boss when things go wrong. Douchebag bosses tend to get bent when things go wrong, and the reason is that they attach too much of their own sense of self-worth to whatever goes wrong, regardless of what it may be. They will spend inordinate amounts of time trying to find someone to blame for the error, especially if the error was theirs. They tend to fix blame before ever considering fixing the problem. Thus is the douchebag nature.

Suspend reasoning: Deciding to stay in this type of work environment requires a special skill set. Do not try to use reason with the situation. That would require the douchebag to make some sort of concession to his bloated ego, and your bringing it up will ultimately make you (in the twisted mind of the douchebag) responsible for it. Nope, your job now is to somehow get him feeling better before he goes around the office charging at things like an African rhino. Remember, the douchebag feels vulnerable in his authority when things go awry—and in any human endeavor things do go wrong. To get his ego off the mindset of fixing blame and onto fixing the problem requires that his ego is pumped back up to its unnatural size. Only then will the douchebag move on to taking care of business, his primary need to feel good about himself being sated.

Whatever went wrong in the office, if the douchebag boss was ultimately responsible—never, ever, bring that up. Tell the douchebag what a great idea it was and how some people can't handle great ideas from great minds. Or tell him that whatever went wrong was because the team under him didn't really understand what was going on, they're not as smart as the douchebag and have a hard tme grasping concepts beyond their peasant mentality. Doing this with a straight face can be the hardest part, but if you really want to keep the job, then so be it.

If something goes wrong at the job and it is your mistake, swallow your own pride and take responsibility for it, and most of all, apologize to the douchebag. That's what he wants to hear so forget about trying to minimize the damage by trying to find mitigating circumstances. In the douchebag boss's mind, you have failed him and made him look bad. Making him look bad is a capital offense. Being penitent after coming clean will also avoid the inevitable witch hunt that the douchebag secretly desires to conduct.

The douchebag cannot differentiate between a real problem and their own problems. A douchebag sees any problem that they have as a universal, all encompassing, crisis of world-shattering proportions. When this happens, it is important to stay in your own bunker of reason and suspend it when dealing with him.

Think out what is going on and determine whether there is truly a problem or the douchebag is having one of his delusional days again. The rule is simple; if there isn't *a* problem, there isn't a problem, so the problem is with the douchebag.

There are two ways to go here.

One, just let the situation slide off you. If you have reasonably determined that nothing is wrong and the douchebag probably had soggy Cheerios for breakfast and he's pissed about it, then just let it go. Don't throw emotional fuel on the fire by pointing out the obvious, reality-based facts. This only serves to make whatever they are going berserker over into a personal struggle. Remember, to a douchebag, just about everything is a personal reflection on themselves, regardless of the reality. Don't challenge them on the point. Even if you win, which is unlikely, in the end you will lose. The douchebag doesn't take kindly to personal rebukes, and they will get you back.

The second option for dealing with the situation is to get on board the psycho train yourself. While your douchebag boss makes his choo choo sounds, you be their whistle. Agree with everything. "Yeah boss, it's horrible," "Yeah boss, they're ruining this country," "Those bastards, they're trying to put us out of business, you're right." It doesn't matter what the situation is or how head-fucked the reasoning, just agree...in spades. Even if you do it in a mocking, condescending tone, the douchebag boss most likely won't be able to tell the difference. They do not have the ablility to empathize and therefore do not understand that you are simply placating them. Their world is wrapped around themselves and all you are doing is agreeing with them. That is all they will see.

Dealing with a douchebag in a general setting: Never openly challenge a douchebag, especially in public. You may win the battle, but they are fighting a war. Usually they are the only one in that war. In public is where the illusion of the douchebag shines, where the flower of their twisted mind is in full bloom. It is also where they are the most vulnerable. To a douchebag, social settings are a treasure trove of new people to impress, new additions to their lineup of other people who will like them for what they are not, new people to fool into thinking them wonderful, clever and the life of the party. They will actively pursue this impression, especially upon the uninitiated; those who don't know the douchebag and can't distinguish the fantasy show they are putting on from the facts of reality. Most people take others at face value, and unless the situation takes a turn for the surreal, most would believe the douchebag and the douchebag's stories.

The douchebag you know: If you know the douchebag in some capacity, don't challenge what they say; it will, even if it is not fully expressed, embarrass them, and of course, it will be you who did the embarrassing. You're gonna pay for it, too. Somewhere down the line the douchebag will find some chink in your armor, some small flaw that he can use to exact a petty revenge for your misplaced words or your chuckle of insolence.

The douchebag you don't know: If the person you're dealing with is someone you do not know, then use your instincts. If the person in question is trying too hard, trying to impress you with their greatness of thought, their superior opinion, or their need to control a conversation by talking over you or getting loud and sometimes over-emotional, then the chances are you're dealing with a douchebag. Remember the signs of a douchebag and how they act.

A good tactic, especially fot those who work in the retail world (although it works in any social situation), is the power of 'OK'. OK is a word that, when used in response to a question, is regarded as an affirmative or agreement.

"Do you want to go to the movies?"

"OK."

It is confirmed that you want to go to the movies. However, in the context of a response to a statement, 'OK' doesn't mean shit.

"This (blah blah blah) isn't what I wanted!"

"OK."

"Those (blah blah blah) are ruining this town (county, state, country, etc.)!"

"OK."

"This is not what I expected!" is especially significant if what they got was from a catalog, brochure, menu, or other type of material that described the item in detail and the individual did not take the time to read it.

"OK"

The phrase 'OK' when used in the face of a demonstrative state-ment, means abosolutely nothing, not in a legal context, or even a social context. But to a douchebag it is disarming. A douchebag is constantly looking for affirmation of everything they say. 'OK' to a douchebag means, in their mind, that you agree. You have stated some form of affirmative that may, quite well, shut them the fuck up. And yet, you have not. At most, you have agreed that they said what they said and nothing more. In most social settings (and especially in jobs that involve dealing with the public) saying 'OK' to stupid statements can get you out of potentially disas-trous situations without having to be embroiled in some douche-bag argument.

You might think sometimes that the best course of action is to call the asshole on his bullshit, but you will never crack the armor that the douchebag has built up to protect himself from such things. Whatever the discussion, his fragile sense of ego will not let him lose and therefore he will change and twist whatever is being dis-cussed into an arena where he will turn any dissent of his point of view into a personal attack, opening up the window to let the emotions fly out, no matter how unemotional the discussion may have been up to that point. To a douchebag, the louder they are, the more right they are. It isn't worth your time. Say 'OK' and walk away.

One of the really fun tactics of a douchebag is emotional baiting. This is a situation where, no matter what transpires, the douche-bag will make it an emotional melee. The reason for this is that the douchebag has found out that the best way to achieve some satisfaction from any situation is to go the childish route. A temper tantrum or crying fit is typical childish behavior and in children is considered somewhat innocuous. It will end, and often end suddenly when the child becomes distracted with something else or gets what the child wants. In adults however, these outbursts can become frightening. A forty-five year old male throwing a temper tantrum can easily lead to violence, and some douchebags habitually use that threat of violence to simply get what they want.

Dealing with this kind of situation takes personal resolve. If you react with anger to the douchebag, you are playing into their hands, into the arena of raw emotion that will solve nothing, save for the fact that they have dragged you into their dark place, where they want you to be emotionally reactive. It is there that they have the power, and you are at the disadvantage.

In these situations it is necessary to stay focused. The douchebag is employing emotional outrage in order to divert you from that focus, to get you off-balance and feeling intimidated. The chink in their armor is that emotional outbursts are considered socially unacceptable, and as long as you do not reciprocate, responsibility falls on the douchebag. In football, it's the guy who hits back who gets the flag. The same applies to dealing with douchebags. Always stay calm. Do not give into the primal instinct of fear that would have you reacting to their emotion, thus making the situation untenable. Stay calm and focus on the singularity of the douchebag's rage and deal with it calmly. Show no emotion; anger only plays into their hands. Smiling (or worse, laughing) can be even more dangerous. These reactions will be perceived as mocking. Showing nothing will frustrate them, because their best tool will have come to no use for them. So stick to the subject and do not react when the douchebag tries to change it to get an upper hand. It's not the Jerry Springer Show. Eventually the douchebag will see the situation as fruitless and walk away, blaming, of course, your complete lack of understanding. So fucking what? Let it go, let them go, and eventually they will.

The trust factor: If you find yourself in the company of someone you know to be or suspect to be a douchebag, never, ever, share personal information with them. Of any kind, of any nature. In typical social relationships sharing personal stories, goals and desires, is a way of bonding, a way in which people come together and strengthen their connection. To a douchebag, none of these things make a damn bit of diffence. Whatever you tell them is filtered through their mind as 'how does this make me look good?' A personal accomplishment on your part is viewed by the douchebag as something that does not boost his own stock, but rather deminishes it by comparison. They lack the ability to be happy for you because they lack empathy – the ability to understand things from the perspective of another. Sharing the small victories of life with a douchebag is a disheartening prospect, and often the douchebag will attempt to minimize or marginalize your success. This is done with subtle or thinly-veiled putdowns, designed not to really disparage you, but to build themselves up in comparison. In the mind of the douchebag, they are the hub of the wheel, and all others are spokes. Your achievement to them is an attempt of the spoke to be a hub, and that to a douchebag, is unacceptable.

Sharing plans or intentions with a douchebag can be a dangerous endeavor. These also will be put down, as your dreams do not aid the douchebag in any way. These will be mocked and derided, usually in a covert manner, sometimes overtly. But they will put down anything that lessens their perceived control. The douchebag once again finds no personal benefit from the dreams of others and he feels a certain threat from those around him who try to excel without him.

In worst case scenarios, sharing personal information with a douchebag will only give them ammunition to use against you. A good example is if you work with a douchebag and are looking for another job. You tell the douchebag this in perceived confidence and then the whole office knows, including the boss. It wasn't so much of a secret, but you really didn't want others knowing you were testing the waters. But you told the douchebag, and the douchebag will swear he didn't tell a soul. Which, of course he did, and that's why the office situation is now very uncomfortable.

But how do you know? How do you realize that a person is a douchebag and would throw you under the bus? Simply listen to them. They will talk about others in the same manner they will talk about you. If one minute they are spewing potentially damaging personal information about someone else, and the next they are smiling in that same person's face, chances are good you're dealing with a douchebag. Cut 'em loose and move on. If you have to deal with them, make sure you protect yourself from them and keep all correspondence in a realm where they cannot get to you.

14

The Kaleidoscope of Douchebag Thinking

Being in the compay of a douchebag at times will invariably mean dealing with psychological anomalies and tactics that the douchebag has in his possession that you should get familiar with. These are the defensive tactics that douchebags use when they feel threatened. Knowing these tactics and understanding them will help keep you on an even keel mentally and emotionally. Don't worry about the douchebag's mental and emotional state, The reality train has left their station a long time ago, so don't hold tickets thinking it'll come back around some day.

Most human interaction, at some point, will have a component of conflict and conflict resolution. These are the everyday issues that arise in the course of life. When dealing with a douchebag, these simple issues can often lead to 'what the fuck was that all about?' moments when a simple conversation takes a turn for the surreal, and a relatively easy, or so you thought, conversation turns into a battle where whatever issue you brought up turns into (in the douchebag's mind) an attack upon their very person.

For the douchebag, the object now becomes a battle to deflect the subject of the disagreement. They have been wounded, not in a physical sense, but rather in the sense of who they think they are. They will attack back. How they do that depends on the severity of the attack.

Here are a few of the tactics the douchebag will use to keep the painful emotions associated with some reality at bay and ways for you to work through it these tactics.

Deflection: Deflection is used to change the subject. When a douchebag feels trapped or cornered he will latch onto some insignificant word or condition in some situation that he feels he is losing at. Then he will blow that insignificant detail out of proportion, and minimize the issue he was losing at. The bigger the douchebag, the more fluid the deflection. Douchebags don't mind doing and saying fucked up shit, but they have a very, very hard time being held accountable for these actions. Their sense of entitlement for themselves says they should be exempt from this sort of thing. If the issue is something that truly *needs* to be addressed, then the best way to overcome this is to dismiss anything the douchebag says that has nothing to do with the subject of the conversation. It will require rigid focus on your part because once the douchebag launches a deflective maneuver and you bite on it, it is hard to get the hook out. It's much less difficult to not allow the douchebag to use deflection than it is to get them to get back to the topic.

This ain't a one-time thing. Once you bring the conversation back to the subject, the douchebag will try a different tactic, some other deflection, some other way around the fence instead of having to actually go over it. Once again, if it is *imperative* to get to the bottom of an issue, keep the conversation on target. Eventually the douchebag will relent and deal with the reality at hand. Yeah, and then the flying pigs come in with the Easter Bunny riding a unicorn. Not likely. Chances are that the conversation will end with personal attacks upon you, aggressive anger, denials, a rewriting of history, and eventually a stomping away. Whatever you do, do not take it personally. It has nothing to do with you; it has everything to do with the douchebag. Allowing the douchebag to ruffle your feathers only lets him get out of the trouble he has put himself in.

Projection: A douchebag is well adept at having flaws in character. He's not truly insane or crazy. Somewhere inside he knows he does the things he does, but when he's doing them it all seems right and all's well with the world. These are not the mistakes that we all make from time to time; these are calculated actions designed to provide the douchebag with some form of personal promotion. He knows somewhere inside that what he does is not good for others, but he can't seem to see that (lack of empathy) when he's doing what he does.

One way a douchebag deals with this is by projection. Unlike deflection, this tactic is a way of dealing with his own twisted psyche and addressing it head first…by accusing someone else of possessing one of his traits. In other words, the douchebag will accuse others of things that the douchebag himself does. For those who do not understand it, projection can be mind boggling, make a person question their own senses, and wonder about the veracity of their own memories. It is the douchebag's way of mind-fucking someone. But once you understand the process—the douchebag dumps on you the things about themselves that they secretly hate—it is easy to see, and to dismiss.

The first step is to have awareness of yourself. Know yourself well enough to keep these attacks from getting a beach-head in your mind. If the douchebag accuses you of being manipulative and controlling, it should be obvious that they are being manipulative and controlling themselves. Without exactly going there, remember the childhood retort of 'I know what you are, but what am I?' This is precisely the situation you are in. Do not react to the douchebag's expressions of projection. Do not defend yourself; it would be useless. Just file it away as another thing you have to deal with because you decided to deal with a douchebag. Being able to understand it will give you more of a grounded place to deal with the douchebag of your choice. Projection is the way douchebags deal with the darker nature of themselves. In this sense, the douchebag places upon you traits of themselves that they subconsciously do not like. Examples would be a cheap douchebag accusing you of being cheap. A judgmental douchebag accusing you of being judgmental. An angry douchebag accusing you of having anger issues. A good line from the poem *If,* by Rudyard Kipling, can summarize this last example:

"If you can keep your head while all about you
Are losing theirs and blaming it on you."

What the douchebag is doing is displacing negative emotional experience that they themselves feel, and projecting them on you.

The douchebag does not have the self-awareness or introspective skills to deal with the emotions themselves, so dumping them on your lap is the next best thing.

Dealing with this particular aspect of the douchebag can be difficult. But if you chose to stay in whatever type of relationship you are in with the douchebag, you had better get used to it, and learn how to deal with it. Dealing with it can be another fun house of mirrors much like dealing with the douchebag's rituals of stupid behavior and then justification.

Understanding the mechanics of projection is a good place to start. Projection can be used in many places. When under attack, the douchebag may use it to derail any conversation where he doesn't like where things are going. Douchebags hate to lose an argument, and projection is a great way to throw it off the rails and get the argument going someplace where the douchebag has a better chance of winning. At the worst, the projection (which to normal people simply seems like an unjustified accusation) will create a defensive mindset. This mindset is an exact mirror of the douchebag, and now he has you on the solid footing of his soft logic. Another way that a douchebag uses projection is simply to bolster his always fragile self-esteem. The projection may seem to come out of nowhere, but to the douchebag it is a way of finding fault in others that helps boost them up from some lower imagined place. It can come in the form of some small slight of insignificant nature or some larger disparagement of your character.

Rationalization: This is another humdinger in the douchebag arsenal. To a certain extent, we all rationalize actions or words to fit ourselves into our own perception of normal. We do this when we speak or act without thinking. It is the knee-jerk response we induce to make a bad situation somehow right, and so we justify the experience. 'Everyone does that or this every now and again' or 'well, it really looked like this or that was the actual situation; anyone would have guessed it the way I did'. For most people, these knee-jerk reactions lessen with age and experience. We grow and realize that most things are not what we think at all, and we wait for the reality to show itself unless immediate action is required.

The douchebag, on the other hand, lives his life in a constant, anxiety-riddled, state of needing to define his world with his powerful tool of assumption, which is always a prerequisite for rationalization. It is not occasional—it is constant. The only time when the douchebag will withhold his assumptions is in the presence of a person who has not been trained to not contradict, and is not open for punishment from the douchebag. Around those the douchebag will hold his tongue and wait for a more receptive audience, and it is here he will need no rationalization.

But rationalization is an aspect of the douchebag that if you intend to remain involved with him, will require careful thought to get through. The douchebag's rationalizations are a bullshit minefield, and if you step on one you're gonna get blown up. The best way to deal with it is to support your douchebag. In his mind he has made a mistake, and that mistake is socially visible, and as we know already, this is a kind of a serious flesh wound to the douchebag. Rationalization is the bandage and the balm. Your job, because you've chosen it, is to help the healing process.

Let him know that whatever he said or did was a brilliant assessment of the situation no matter how fucked up or just plain stupid it was. Do not make it look like you're coming to his rescue. The douchebag doesn't want that; it makes him look feeble. But be supportive of whatever bullshit justification comes out of his mouth…it'll make your life easier. Any other reaction will cause reprisals, somewhere, someday.

Douchebag debunking: Depending on what you have to lose from any situation with a douchebag will determine how you deal with it. Remember, the douchebag is in a constant battle to keep his false impression of himself up to par, especially in the face of reality which will tend to not be kind to his false self.

One way *not* to deal with it is to get angry. That, once again, will put you on the emotional, nonsensical footing that the douchebag loves. Instead, ask for instances or facts of the accusations mentioned. Typically, the douchebag will have none but will try to defend his statement, usually with a combination of misdirection, change of subject, or scare tactics designed to stop the siege. Either way, you may be able to keep the projections at bay by challenging them. Like justifications, the more the douchebag learns that he cannot get away with it with you, the less he will do it to you, and then he can go on to some other poor slob who will buy into the bullshit.

On the other hand, if you've been down that road before, and that road has run you into some form of retribution for your obvious transgressions, you may want to simply understand where it's coming from and just let it slide. Agree with the douchebag, ask for help in how to change and become better. This will be the equivalent of stroking his emotional penis and it will bring him pleasure. But just like all the other subterfuges you need to perform to keep a reasonable sanity in any relationship with a douchebag...try not to laugh.

15

The Douchebag Mutual Admiration Society

Douchebags have an innate sense of when they are around their own kind. They will find each other in a group the same way two cinematic lovers find each other in a crowded room. The reason is that a douchebag senses when he can be his douchebag self and not have to hold himself to any better standard than that. Among his douchebag peers he can allow his self-absorbed nature to take on the auspices of a Mardi gras parade without fear of awkward questions as to the intent of his statements, because they all make perfect sense to other douchebags. They can use their 'gathering of the douches' to make fun of others, to bolster their own soap-bubble egos, to compliment each other as the greatest, the best. They will tell each other that the stupid shit they do in life is truly not their fault – they were robbed, cheated somehow, of the greatness that eludes them. This gives the douchebag a feeling of security in a frightful world where reality diminishes their impossible dreams that they never had the self-discipline to pursue. It is a grand circle-jerk of bullshit and ego-stroking.

Your douchebag will seek out such gatherings, places where he will not be challenged and can act like the juvenile he really is inside. When he returns from such gatherings, he will be energized by his delusions, and by the company of others who share (if not the same then similar) delusions of grandeur.

In addition to the mutual admiration society, the douchebag will also be energized by other events that help him to elevate his stature. He may have just maliciously undermined some perceived competitor, or lied to someone who believed him. Whatever happened, it has boosted his fragile self-esteem, and he flies high.

This is not the time to try to bring him back to reality or let him in on what he really might have done. The bubble of his false self is so large after such encounters and events that it, like any bubble growing large, is ready to pop. Do not be the one to do it. Leave him be. Agree with whatever comes out of his mouth, no matter how ridiculous it may seem. With a little time and luck, your douchebag will allow the bubble to deflate to its normal (yet still reality-challenged) size. Let him spend some time in his land where the unicorns shit rainbows and he is the power to be dealt with. He may even be in a better mood, and this could be the time to try to press some issue that you were afraid to discuss while the douchebag was in his normal state of insecurity. In this state of temporary euphoria, the douchebag is also vulnerable, and taking advantage of it is a way to even out the playing field. This may sound a bit Machiavellian, but after periods of walking on egg shells it may be the time to get what *you* want from the relationship, and the window doesn't last long, so run, don't walk.

16

The Douchebag Anti-Defamation League

Another aspect of the douchebag mutual admiration society is the douchebag anti-defamation leauge. Just as the douchebag will find a shallow high from being among those who really understand him and his fucked-up shit, he will also come to the aid and be supportive of those who express themselves in a fucked-up way. They know what it is like to have such a loose sense of self-control over themselves and will defend it in others. In reality, he is only defending himself and his own weaknesses. So when you have some strange experience with some other douchebag, don't expect your own personal douchebag to be there with a shoulder to lean on. Don't even think of going to him with such things and remember that that is another aspect of your choice to remain in a relationship with a douchebag. His world is an exaggerated emotional one where reason and logic do not exist (remember the unicorns), and that world is constantly under attack from the world of truth and fact. It will be defended in others because in reality he is defending it in himself.

17

Attack of the Martyr Douchebags

Then there's the douchebags who, being not wholly in control of themselves, wish to control others. One of the ways they will do this (if there is a form of relationship) or will test the waters (if there is no relationship), is by playing the martyr. These emotional vampire types of douchebags want you to be responsible, or to take blame for something that they feel. In work settings, they will personalize a reprimand, feel crappy about it and blame the reprimander, no matter how well deserved the criticism. In personal relationships, you will always let them down, no matter how hard you work. The martyr douchbag tries to manipulate the thoughts of others by claiming the high ground of victim, a favorite American pastime, and placing others below them either in an ethical or moral setting.

The one good thing about dealing with the martyr douchebag is that it is fairly easy to disarm them, but it again requires awareness and consciousness in dealing with them. After a while of practice, they will either cease throwing themselves up on their cross of hurt feeling like an Olympic high jumper or they will leave you alone knowing full well that you will challenge their position of being aggrieved in some way.

First and foremost, when dealing with someone whom you know or suspect to be a martyr type of douchebag, *you* need to be specific in what you say and aware of what you do. This means making sure that the words you speak are clear and in no way derogatory or could possibly be interpreted that way, and that what you are doing cannot be taken out of context. A douchebag is looking for any type of slip on your part to get themselves up on their cross. If a martyr type douchebag asks for something that you do not wish to give or do something you cannot do, simply say 'no'. Say 'no' without explanation or reason. Explanation and reason are the Petri dish where the douchebag virus thrives. Any reason you give will be met with some form of counter by the douchebag who needs – *needs* – to have what he wants. If a douchebag sees you doing something and they take it out of context, ignore their remarks (most likely it's projection anyway). When it comes to asking the martyr questions, keep the questions close ended. In other words, do not ask them what they want, tell them what is available and let them know these are the choices they have and no more. Being firm in this manner will keep the douchebag from going 'off the board' into a realm where their fantasy choices are not allowed. In these matters, it is a very good idea to limit options to the point where you leave the douchebag with a 'yes' or 'no' choice. Think of it as if you were dealing with children (douchebags are children on an emotional level) and being a martyr is just another tactic. If you try to be too kind and ask them what they want and they ask for a pony, then you are on the hook for not getting them a pony...you insensitive bastard.

There will always be a time when a douchebag, completely out of touch with reality, will blame you for making them feel a certain way. These are the douchebags known as the merchants of guilt. If you have followed the rules of speaking clearly and plainly (without the possibility of derogatory implication) and your actions have not impeded upon the douchebag, then the problem they have is their problem. Don't give into it and remember that you are responsible for your own words and actions, but not responsible for their feelings. The first time you capitulate on this reasoning, you give the douchebag emotionally fertile soil to plant their seeds of bullshit. Don't be the soil.

Another type of martyr douchebag is the *giving* douchebag. These are the douchebags who will do things for you or bestow gifts where there are strings attached. For the record, a gift, a *true* gift, is given freely with no expectation of return, not even a thank you. A martyr douchebag has no concept of this; everything they do in life, everything they have done, has revolved around doing for others for the sake of some return at a later date. This is not giving, no matter how much they may think themselves deserving of return for such actions. To do for others and expect something in return is simply, and only, a business transaction.

18

The Anti-Douchebag Toolbox

Dealing with douchebags can be a nerve-wracking, soul-draining, mind-blowing experience as many who have done so can tell you. They are manipulative and self-centered to the extreme. They are the arrogant, smug, and self-absorbed of the world where they are their only concern...unless of course, you can do something for them. They lack basic empathy – no matter how sympathetic or compassionate they appear – and they are everywhere. They are the holdovers from childhood, the Peter Pans who refuse to grow up and work to drag you down. You will meet one tomorrow and you will meet one again the day after. You cannot rid the world of them, and sometimes they have a lot of control over the world (or think they should, anyway). Even if you have a job or a social situation where you do not have to deal with them constantly, hopefuly this book has given you some knowledge of what to look for before you become embroiled with one – or worse – many. If you do have to engage with them, in business or if you deal with the general public, hopefully this book has given you some strategies, a toolbox of sorts, for keeping your own sanity while among them. Douchebags like disorder among others; it gives them a better sense of their illusion of control, and being able to recognize one at the outset will help to lessen that control. But in the end the goal will be to leave these people in the rear view mirror. As much as you may think that particular tactic a bit harsh, sometimes in life you need to gather around you those who help you to inspire yourself to be the best you can and let go of those who would drag you down. Douchebags do not have the ability to inspire; it is lost to them, but they have tremendous abilities to drag you down, because dragging others down elevates themselves by comparison, leaving you in the lurch somehow. They do not have the capacity for true change, because they think they are already on the right track and whatever negative personal qualities they do possess (and grudgingly admit to) are marginalized or justified. They are stuck on a juvenile plane of existence for whatever reason, and even though you will see glimpses of hope every now and then (thinking that it is progress) it will be short lived, and you will once again lose something in the bargain.

Understanding the douchebag and realizing what's going on can help us also to understand ourselves a little better and recognize that there's a little douche bag—if we have the strength to admit it—in us all. But only when we can see, when we can realize that some of the things we consider traits of our personality, are simply habits that we have allowed to go on for too long, or habits that do not serve us in being a better human beings and becoming more successful in our lives. By acknowledging bad habits in ourselves and refusing to justify them with a simple 'well it's just the way I am' we give ourselves the opportunity to rise above and work on the things that truly matter in our lives and help us from living an unconscicous life.

No one in this world is perfect; we all have things we can work on. Accepting douchebags in your life will not help you in that endeavor, nor is accepting in yourself traits that serve no one but who you think you are.

The douchebag apocalypse is upon us, and it shows no sign of stopping, but we can be prepared. If you've read this book and come to the conclusion that you see a great deal of yourself in it, but didn't realize it before, there's hope. Awareness is the first step to overcoming and achieving. If you're a real douche bag (and that would be doubtful because a real douchebag would have angrily thrown this book away or simply would have stopped reading a long way back) then you're doing a literary version of putting your hands over your ears and making a humming sound that will drown out what you have read.

You just don't want to hear it.

Hopefully this book has left you with a greater sense of understanding of some of the darker aspects of human nature and ways to cope with the sometimes horrible people who exhibit these traits, and especially if sometimes that horrible person looks back at you in the mirror.

CPSIA information can be obtained at www.ICGtesting.com
Printed in the USA
BVOW06s0814200815

414262BV00012B/131/P

9 781478 722564